Catholic Action in America

C. A. Chuba

VITAE PRESS
EMBARK ON YOUR QUEST

ISBN: 978-1-967470-17-4

Published by Vitae Press LLC

Cover design by C. A. Chuba

Vitae Press

Vitae Press is a publishing house dedicated to exploring the enduring legacy of Western life, thought, and culture as shaped by the Roman tradition. The name *Vitae*, derived from the Latin word for "life," reflects our mission to publish works that engage with the values, ideas, and heritage of the Western world. From fiction to non-fiction to reprints of timeless works from Christendom and Western Civilization, each book seeks to deepen the understanding of the moral, spiritual, and intellectual foundations that have guided generations and continue to inspire today.

TABLE OF CONTENTS

ACKNOWLEDGMENT

This work is written in the hope that the generations who follow us may inherit a Catholic society capable of sustaining their faith, their families, and their communities. In a particular way it is written for my son, *Austin Deane Chuba*, and for any other children that my wife and I may be blessed to raise in the years to come. May they grow up within a diocese that is strong in its institutions, confident in its identity, and faithful in its mission. May the Church that surrounds them provide the protection, formation, and fellowship necessary to stand firmly within the faith while living faithfully in a secular age. If the efforts described in these pages contribute even in a small way to the renewal of such a Catholic society, then the work will have served its purpose.

INTRODUCTION

✠ A CALL TO CATHOLIC ACTION IN AMERICA ✠

The present moment is often described as a time of rapid cultural change. Yet it may be more accurate to say that we are living through something deeper and more troubling. Many of the signs point not simply to cultural transition but to a genuine civilizational crisis.

Across much of the Western world the institutions that once gave shape and coherence to human life are weakening. The family, which for centuries served as the primary school of love, responsibility, and moral formation, has become increasingly fragile. Birth rates decline across developed nations, suggesting not only demographic change but also a quiet loss of confidence in the future. At the same time many communities experience rising levels of loneliness, addiction, and despair. Though surrounded by constant communication and technological connectivity, large numbers of people experience a profound sense of isolation.

Modern culture frequently proposes a vision of freedom detached from the structures that once gave it meaning. The permanence of marriage is often dismissed as unrealistic, while patterns of promiscuity are presented as expressions of personal autonomy. Entire industries now thrive upon pornography and sexual exploitation in a digital environment where such material can be accessed instantly and without restraint. What was once confined to the margins of society has entered the mainstream of cultural life, shaping the imagination of entire generations.

Other forms of vice have likewise expanded through modern entertainment networks. Gambling spreads through cities, sports industries, and digital platforms, promising excitement or sudden wealth while quietly fostering habits of dependence and financial ruin. Meanwhile the entertainment economy fills nearly every hour of life with images, stimulation, and narrative worlds that gradually reshape the moral imagination of those who consume them.

Technologies designed for convenience and communication increasingly dominate the hours that once belonged to prayer, family life, shared conversation, and meaningful work. The rhythms of human life slowly begin to conform not to the deeper needs of the soul but to the demands of technology, distraction, and entertainment.

A civilization that once organized itself around God, family, and community now drifts toward isolation, distraction, and moral confusion. Sacred Scripture long ago warned of the consequences that follow when societies abandon the moral order. The Book of Judges describes such a moment with striking simplicity: "In those days there was no king in Israel:

but every one did that which seemed right to himself."[1]

At the same time the destruction of unborn life continues on a scale that would have been unimaginable to earlier generations. Millions of children who should have been welcomed into the world are never given the chance to live. A society that permits such a tragedy cannot honestly claim to defend the dignity of the human person. The Christian tradition has always insisted that the value of human life does not arise from social usefulness or personal autonomy, but from the fact that each human being is created in the image of God.

Nor is the destruction of unborn life the only sign of moral disorder. Over recent generations practices that once stood clearly outside the Christian moral framework have gradually been normalized and even celebrated. Divorce has become widespread, the permanence of marriage increasingly questioned, and sexual ethics that earlier societies understood as essential to family stability are now frequently presented as restrictions upon personal freedom.

The moral imagination of modern society has drifted so far from the Christian understanding of the human person that even the warnings preserved in Scripture are often dismissed as relics of an unenlightened past. Yet the ancient prophets spoke with remarkable clarity about the

---

[1] The Holy Bible, Translated from the Latin Vulgate, Douay-Rheims Edition (Baltimore: John Murphy Company, A.D. 1899), Judges 21:25.

danger of moral inversion. As the prophet Isaiah warned, "Woe to you that call evil good, and good evil: that put darkness for light, and light for darkness."[2]

Earlier generations trembled at the story of Sodom and Gomorrah. Yet even those cities, condemned in Scripture for their corruption, did not attempt to institutionalize what modern societies increasingly celebrate as law.

These developments arise within the same civilization that possesses immense industrial and technological power. The twentieth century revealed with frightening clarity what such power can produce when it becomes detached from moral restraint. Industrial economies manufactured weapons on a scale previously unimaginable, and fleets of aircraft carried those weapons across continents and oceans. Cities that once contained ordinary families living their daily lives suddenly became targets of vast military campaigns conducted from the sky.

Bombs fell in such numbers that entire districts disappeared beneath fire and smoke. And those bombs did not fall upon armies alone. They fell upon cities filled with civilians, women, children, the elderly, and the disabled, while the soldiers of those nations fought on distant front lines. During the Second World War entire German cities were subjected to

---

[2] The Holy Bible, Translated from the Latin Vulgate, Douay-Rheims Edition (Baltimore: John Murphy Company, A.D. 1899), Isaiah 5:20.

massive campaigns of aerial bombardment in which explosives and incendiaries produced devastating firestorms. In the final months of that same war two atomic bombs were dropped upon the Japanese cities of Hiroshima and Nagasaki, unleashing a destructive force previously unknown in human history and killing tens of thousands of civilians within moments.

The Christian tradition has long warned that power separated from moral truth becomes destructive. As St. Augustine observed when reflecting on the political orders of history, "Justice being taken away, then, what are kingdoms but great robberies?"[3]

✠ ✠ ✠

The result is a strange contradiction. Our civilization possesses immense technological power and material wealth, yet many individuals experience a profound sense of disconnection and purposelessness. Modern society has extended its mastery over nature, multiplied its productive capacity, and filled daily life with devices that promise convenience, speed, and entertainment. Yet beneath this remarkable progress there remains a growing spiritual emptiness.

Entertainment expands while meaning contracts. Communication technologies multiply while genuine community becomes more difficult to

---

[3] St. Augustine, *The City of God*. Translated by Marcus Dods. New York: Random House, A.D. 1950. Book IV, Chapter 4.

sustain. The modern individual is surrounded by constant stimulation, yet often experiences a quiet and persistent isolation. A culture capable of projecting images instantly across the globe struggles to preserve the human bonds that once held together families, neighborhoods, and communities.

The Christian tradition has long recognized the deeper source of such restlessness. The human person was not created merely for comfort, productivity, or diversion. Man was created for communion with God. As St. Augustine wrote at the beginning of his *Confessions*, "Thou hast made us for Thyself, O Lord, and our heart is restless until it rests in Thee."[4]

This contradiction reveals a deeper problem. Technological advancement does not guarantee moral advancement. A society may become extraordinarily skilled in the manipulation of matter while gradually losing clarity about the purpose of human life itself. When this occurs, progress in technique can exist alongside confusion in morality. Immense power may accumulate in a civilization that has lost confidence in the moral principles that ought to guide it.

Sacred Scripture warns that material success alone cannot satisfy the deepest needs of the human person. Christ Himself posed the question with striking simplicity: "What doth it profit a man, if he gain the whole

---

[4] St. Augustine, *Confessions*. Translated by E. B. Pusey (London: John Henry Parker, A.D. 1838), Book I, Chapter 1.

world, and suffer the loss of his own soul?"[5]

A civilization that loses its moral compass rarely loses its power at the same time. More often it retains that power and continues to expand it, though increasingly without direction. When strength becomes detached from justice, political and economic power can become destructive both to others and to the society that wields it. Sacred Scripture reminds us that "Justice exalteth a nation: but sin maketh nations miserable."[6]

This observation does not imply that everything produced by American civilization is corrupt or without merit. Many of the most admirable features of American society emerged precisely from the influence of its Christian inheritance. The moral imagination shaped by Christianity helped inspire institutions of charity, education, law, and civic responsibility. Wherever that influence has remained strong, American society has often displayed remarkable energy, generosity, and creativity.

Yet when a society slowly departs from its moral foundation, its power does not disappear. On the contrary, its technical capacity often continues to grow even as the principles that once guided its use begin to fade. The result is a civilization capable of extraordinary achievement, yet increasingly uncertain about the moral direction of its own institutions.

---

[5] The Holy Bible, Translated from the Latin Vulgate, Douay-Rheims Edition (Baltimore: John Murphy Company, A.D. 1899), Matthew 16:26.
[6] The Holy Bible, Translated from the Latin Vulgate, Douay-Rheims Edition (Baltimore: John Murphy Company, A.D. 1899), Proverbs 14:34.

Within such an environment Catholics face a particular challenge.

✠ ✠ ✠

Throughout Christian history the primary structure through which Christian civilization was organized was the diocese. A diocese is not simply an administrative division of the Church. It is a living community of faith gathered around a bishop and rooted in a particular place. Within its boundaries parishes, families, schools, and institutions are united in a common spiritual and social life. Through this structure the Church has historically served not only as a place of worship but also as a center of culture, charity, education, and economic cooperation.

From the earliest centuries of Christianity, the unity of the faithful around the bishop was understood to be essential to the life of the Church. Writing in the third century, St. Cyprian of Carthage expressed this principle with striking clarity: "The Church is in the bishop and the bishop is in the Church; and if anyone is not with the bishop, he is not in the Church."[7]

Seen in this light, the diocese may be understood as one of the foundational structures through which Christian civilization itself developed. Wherever the Church established stable diocesan life, Christian society gradually formed around it. Parishes became the center of local

---

[7] St. Cyprian of Carthage, *Epistle 66*. In *The Ante-Nicene Fathers*, Volume 5 (Buffalo: Christian Literature Publishing Co., A.D. 1886).

communities. Guilds organized economic activity. Charitable institutions cared for the poor, the sick, and the vulnerable. Schools formed new generations in the faith and transmitted the intellectual inheritance of Christian culture. Through the life of the diocese Christian civilization was able to reproduce itself across generations.

The Catechism of the Catholic Church expresses this reality clearly: "A diocese is a portion of the People of God which is entrusted to a bishop to be shepherded by him with the cooperation of the presbyterate."[8]

For generations the Church in the United States has built remarkable institutions of charity and service. Across the country stand Catholic hospitals, pregnancy centers, food banks, shelters, schools, and universities. Catholic volunteers feed the hungry, care for the sick, and support families in moments of crisis. These works remain among the most visible expressions of Christian charity in the modern world.

Yet these works of mercy exist within an even broader network of Catholic life. Catholic schools educate millions of children. Catholic universities form the minds of future leaders. Parish communities sustain the sacramental life of the faithful. Catholic charities, fraternal organizations, investment groups, and insurance societies operate throughout the country. For generations Catholics have devoted their labor,

---

[8] Catechism of the Catholic Church (Vatican City: Libreria Editrice Vaticana, A.D. 1992), §833.

their resources, and their faith to building institutions capable of sustaining both the spiritual and material life of their communities.

Taken together, this network represents one of the most extensive religious infrastructures in the nation. Few religious communities possess such a wide system of schools, charitable institutions, social organizations, and cultural traditions. The Church in America has inherited resources, talent, and institutional experience of extraordinary scale.

And yet this inheritance has not produced the kind of coherent Catholic social life that earlier generations believed possible. The institutions remain, but the sense of a living Catholic civilization has weakened. Catholics continue to participate in many of these institutions, yet much of their daily life is increasingly shaped by structures that exist entirely outside them.

It is possible for a community to preserve its institutions while gradually losing the spirit that once animated them. Structures may remain long after the conviction, unity, and missionary zeal that originally gave them life have begun to fade. Sacred Scripture records such a warning in the message addressed to the early Christian community at Ephesus. Though that Church still possessed its works, its reputation, and its visible organization, Christ rebuked it for a deeper loss within its heart: "But I have somewhat against thee, because thou hast left thy first charity."[9]

✠ ✠ ✠

For many Catholics today the Church exists primarily as a place they attend rather than a society in which they live. The Catholic faith shapes the hour spent at Mass on Sunday, yet the remaining days of the week unfold within structures that bear little relation to the Christian understanding of man and society.

The difficulties facing the Church are therefore not only external. They are also visible within Catholic life itself. In many places catechesis has weakened to such an extent that large numbers of baptized Catholics no longer understand or believe central teachings of the faith. Surveys repeatedly show that many who identify as Catholic do not believe in the Real Presence of Christ in the Eucharist, the sacrament that stands at the very center of Catholic worship. The Church has always taught the centrality of the Eucharist to Christian life. As the Catechism of the Catholic Church states, "The Eucharist is the source and summit of the Christian life."[10]

At the same time numerous dioceses across the United States face a shortage of priests and rely increasingly on clergy from countries where

---

[9] The Holy Bible, Translated from the Latin Vulgate, Douay-Rheims Edition (Baltimore: John Murphy Company, A.D. 1899), Revelation 2:4.
[10] Catechism of the Catholic Church (Vatican City: Libreria Editrice Vaticana, A.D. 1992), §1324.

the faith remains more vibrant. This reality does not reflect a failure on the part of those priests who generously serve the Church abroad. Rather it reveals that the Christian culture which once sustained Catholic life in America has weakened significantly. The structures that once formed and supported the faith no longer function as they once did.

Young Catholics are still baptized, educated, and formed within the Church. Their families bring them to the sacraments. They attend parish schools or youth ministries. They serve at the altar and learn the prayers of the faith. Many receive an education that introduces them to the moral tradition of Christianity and to the intellectual inheritance of Western civilization.

Yet when they enter adulthood their lives are quickly absorbed into a world built upon different foundations. Their labor is given to corporations whose primary concern is profit rather than the common good. Their savings flow into financial systems whose operations remain distant and impersonal. Their daily habits are shaped by technologies and cultural industries that rarely encourage reflection, sacrifice, or lasting community.

This separation between Catholic life and the structures of society becomes especially visible in the economic systems that shape daily life. Many Catholics deposit their savings in financial institutions that invest those funds in industries and political movements that openly contradict

Christian moral teaching. Health insurance programs, investment funds, and corporate financial networks often support practices such as abortion, contraception, and other policies incompatible with the moral tradition of the Church. In this way, ordinary Catholics may unintentionally finance institutions whose goals conflict with their own beliefs.

At the same time the economic life of many communities has been hollowed out. Local businesses disappear while national corporations expand into every town and city. Workers become increasingly dependent upon large institutions that offer little connection to the communities in which they operate. Families accumulate debt through financial systems that benefit distant economic centers while local economies struggle to sustain small businesses and independent trades.

The consequences of this separation are increasingly visible. Catholics continue to worship together on Sunday, yet much of their labor, wealth, and daily life remains embedded within structures that neither recognize nor support the moral vision of the Church. Financial systems, media industries, and cultural institutions increasingly shape the habits and imaginations of society in ways that weaken family life, encourage vice, and undermine Christian culture.

These developments reveal that the problem facing the Church today is not limited to individual moral failure. It is structural. The institutions that organize modern life increasingly operate according to principles that stand in tension with the Christian understanding of the human person. Catholic social teaching has long warned against such conditions. As Pope Pius XI observed, the modern economy tends toward a dangerous concentration of power in the hands of large institutions: "This concentration of power and might has produced a threefold struggle for domination: first, for dictatorship in the economic sphere itself; then for control over the State."[11]

If Catholic communities are to flourish within such an environment, they must gradually rebuild networks of cooperation capable of sustaining their social, economic, and cultural life.

In many cases, the present arrangement is accepted simply because it appears inevitable. The economic, technological, and cultural systems of modern life appear so vast that individuals assume they have no alternative but to participate in them as they exist. The result is a quiet fragmentation of life in which faith becomes one compartment among many rather than the principle that orders the whole.

Sacred Scripture warns believers not to conform themselves to such conditions: "And be not conformed to this world; but be reformed in the newness of your mind."[12]

On Sunday Catholics pray the words taught by Christ Himself:

---

[11] Pope Pius XI, *Quadragesimo Anno* (Vatican City: Vatican City Press, A.D. 1931), §109.
[12] The Holy Bible, Translated from the Latin Vulgate, Douay-Rheims Edition (Baltimore: John Murphy Company, A.D. 1899), Romans 12:2.

"Thy kingdom come, Thy will be done on earth as it is in heaven."[13]

Yet on Monday morning they often return to institutions governed by a different set of assumptions, repeating the language and priorities of a secular society in which liberty and equality are frequently spoken of with a reverence that once belonged to God.

✠ ✠ ✠

Meanwhile the Church's charitable institutions continue their work faithfully. They feed the hungry, shelter the homeless, assist the struggling, and comfort the abandoned. These works remain sacred and indispensable expressions of Christian love. Sacred Scripture repeatedly commands such acts of mercy: "For I was hungry, and you gave me to eat: I was thirsty, and you gave me to drink: I was a stranger, and you took me in."[14]

Yet charity alone cannot sustain a civilization.

The mission of the Church has always been broader than the relief of suffering. Christianity does not merely comfort the wounded after society has failed them. It seeks to shape the conditions of life so that human dignity is protected from the beginning. The apostles themselves understood this mission clearly. They did not limit their work to acts of charity among scattered communities. St. Peter and St. Paul carried the

[13] The Holy Bible, Translated from the Latin Vulgate, Douay-Rheims Edition (Baltimore: John Murphy Company, A.D. 1899), Matthew 6:10.
[14] The Holy Bible, Translated from the Latin Vulgate, Douay-Rheims Edition (Baltimore: John Murphy Company, A.D. 1899), Matthew 25:35.

Gospel to Rome, the very center of imperial power, seeking not only to convert individuals but to bring the light of Christ into the heart of the civilization that governed the world. From the earliest centuries the Church understood that the moral order of society must serve the common good. As St. Thomas Aquinas later wrote, "The common good of the multitude is more divine and more to be sought than the good of the individual."[15]

For centuries, Catholic societies built institutions that reflected this conviction. Guilds organized economic life. Parishes formed the center of community life. Families, schools, and workplaces existed within a shared moral framework that reinforced the dignity of the human person and the responsibilities of the community. The faith was not confined to private devotion but extended into the structures that governed work, commerce, education, and public life.

The principles that sustained such societies were not accidental. They reflected the social philosophy developed within the Catholic tradition itself. The Church consistently taught that social life should be ordered according to the principles of subsidiarity, solidarity, and the common good. Economic life was meant to be widely distributed among families and local communities rather than concentrated in distant monopolies, an idea

---

[15] St Thomas Aquinas, *Summa Theologiae*. Translated by the Fathers of the English Dominican Province (New York: Benziger Brothers, A.D. 1947. I–II, q.90, a.2.

later articulated by Catholic thinkers as Distributism.[16] Likewise the historic unity between spiritual authority and the moral ordering of society reflected the long-standing Christian conviction that faith and public life cannot be permanently separated without damaging both.

Catholic social teaching has repeatedly affirmed these principles. As Pope Pius XI wrote in *Quadragesimo Anno*, "It is an injustice and at the same time a grave evil to assign to a greater and higher association what lesser and subordinate organizations can do."[17]

In practical terms this meant that Christian communities sought to develop and maintain their own institutions whenever possible. The talents of their people, the organizations they built, the land they cultivated, and the resources they accumulated were directed toward strengthening the life of the local Church itself. Personnel, technology, economic assets, and charitable institutions were organized within the life of the diocese so that the community could sustain its spiritual, social, and economic responsibilities without excessive dependence upon distant structures that did not share its moral vision.

That unity has largely disappeared in the modern age.

Today many Catholics spend the majority of their waking hours

---

[16] *Distributism*: is the Catholic social principle that productive property should be broadly owned by families and local communities rather than concentrated in either corporate monopolies or centralized state control.
[17] Pope Pius XI, *Quadragesimo Anno* (Vatican City: Vatican Press, A.D. 1931), §79.

working within institutions that neither recognize nor prioritize the moral vision of the Church. Their talents, education, and creativity serve structures whose ultimate purposes are often defined only by profit, efficiency, or political power. What once functioned as a coherent Christian civilization has gradually dissolved into a society in which faith survives primarily as a private practice rather than a public organizing principle.

Sacred Scripture warns believers against such a separation between faith and life: "Faith, if it have not works, is dead in itself."[18]

✠ ✠ ✠

Yet the tragedy of this situation is not that Catholics lack ability or resources. The tragedy is that the necessary pieces already exist.

Across the country stand magnificent cathedrals and parish churches built by generations who believed that the faith could shape an entire civilization. Catholic schools continue to educate millions of students. Catholic universities train men and women in fields ranging from engineering and medicine to business, law, and science. Within parishes and Catholic organizations there exists an enormous reserve of talent. Teachers, builders, entrepreneurs, engineers, farmers, doctors, artists, and scholars possess the ability to build institutions that reflect Catholic principles.

The infrastructure exists. The tradition exists. The people exist.

---

[18] The Holy Bible, Translated from the Latin Vulgate, Douay-Rheims Edition (Baltimore: John Murphy Company, A.D. 1899), James 2:17.

What is often missing is coordination and vision.

This work cannot be accomplished by any single individual. The Church is not built by isolated effort but by communities of believers who labor together within their vocations. Each person devotes much of his time and energy to the responsibilities of family and profession. Yet when those individuals unite their skills and resources within a shared framework, their combined efforts can build institutions far greater than anything a single person could accomplish alone.

Sacred Scripture emphasizes the strength that arises from such cooperation: "It is better therefore that two should be together than one: for they have the advantage of their society."[19]

The Church herself has always understood her life in this way. St. Paul describes the Christian community as a living body composed of many members working together for a common purpose: "For as the body is one, and hath many members; and all the members of the body, whereas they are many, yet are one body, so also is Christ."[20]

Nothing great in human history has been accomplished by individuals acting alone, nor by vague global movements without roots. The great works of civilization have always been built by disciplined

[19] The Holy Bible, Translated from the Latin Vulgate, Douay-Rheims Edition (Baltimore: John Murphy Company, A.D. 1899), Ecclesiastes 4:9.
[20] The Holy Bible, Translated from the Latin Vulgate, Douay-Rheims Edition (Baltimore: John Murphy Company, A.D. 1899), 1 Corinthians 12:12.

communities of faithful men and women working patiently together across generations. Such cooperation will be required of any diocese that seeks the renewal proposed in these pages.

History also reveals another lesson. When governments detach themselves from the moral framework that once sustained them, they rarely become neutral or harmless. Over time they tend to become unstable. Political orders that separate themselves from the Christian vision of the human person often grow increasingly confused about the purpose of their own authority. Eventually such systems become destructive not only to others but also to themselves.

The experience of the late Western Roman Empire offers a powerful example. The imperial order passed through periods of hostility toward the Church, political corruption, social fragmentation, and finally collapse under the pressures of internal decay and external invasion. Yet when imperial authority disintegrated, the Church did not disappear with it. What remained were the dioceses, the parishes, and the networks of Christian communities that continued to organize social life after the empire had failed. From those structures the foundations of Western civilization were gradually rebuilt.

A similar lesson confronts the present age. The Catholic institutions that exist in America today perform extraordinary charitable and educational work, yet they do not yet form a coordinated social structure capable of sustaining Christian civilization on their own. If Christian society is to endure through the uncertainties of the modern age, the Church must once again cultivate stronger networks of cooperation within her own life. The parish, the diocese, and the institutions connected to them must become centers not only of worship and charity but also of centralized social organization.

Recent years have also revealed how fragile the cultural position of Christianity has become. Churches that once stood peacefully at the center of civic life have been vandalized, burned, or attacked. Sacred spaces built through the sacrifices of earlier generations are increasingly treated as relics of a past that many modern institutions would prefer to forget. Such events should dispel any lingering illusion that Catholic communities can assume their institutions will always be respected or protected by the surrounding culture.

For this reason, Catholics must once again take seriously the responsibility of safeguarding what has been entrusted to them. The protection of churches, schools, and families is not an act of hostility toward others. It is an act of stewardship. Communities that cherish what is sacred must be prepared to organize responsibly for its protection through vigilance, training, and cooperation with lawful authorities.

Sacred Scripture offers an image that captures this responsibility with striking clarity. When the people of Jerusalem rebuilt their city, they labored together with vigilance and determination: "They that built the wall, and they that carried burdens... with one hand they wrought in the work, and with the other they held a sword."[21]

A civilization that forgets how to build and protect its churches may soon discover that it can no longer keep them.

At the same time, young Catholics possess skills that previous generations did not. They understand digital communication, online networks, and new forms of collaboration. They bring energy, creativity, and technical knowledge that could renew Catholic institutions for a new century.

✠ ✠ ✠

What is needed, therefore, is not the abandonment of the Church's charitable mission but its expansion. The works of mercy must remain at the heart of Christian life, yet they must be supported by institutions capable of shaping the conditions of society itself. Charity can relieve suffering, but a civilization guided by Christian principles can prevent much of that suffering from arising in the first place.

Catholic Action means the renewal of Catholic life in its fullness. It means that the talents of the faithful are not confined solely to charitable works but extend into the shaping of economic, cultural, and social

---

[21] The Holy Bible, Translated from the Latin Vulgate, Douay-Rheims Edition (Baltimore: John Murphy Company, A.D. 1899), Nehemiah 4:17.

institutions. It means building networks of cooperation among Catholics so that the faith does not remain isolated within private devotion but becomes visible within the structures of everyday life.

Pope Pius XI defined *Catholic Action* as "the collaboration of the laity in the apostolate of the hierarchy."[22] In this sense *Catholic Action* refers to the organized participation of ordinary Catholics in the mission of the Church, not only through personal devotion but through the deliberate ordering of their work, institutions, and communities according to the principles of the Christian faith.

Catholic Action therefore does not mean the pursuit of power for its own sake, nor does it require the creation of entirely new political movements. Rather, it means the ordered cooperation of Catholics within the ordinary structures of life. Parents form their children in the faith. Teachers shape minds according to truth. Business owners organize their enterprises according to principles of justice and stewardship. Professionals bring the moral vision of the Church into the fields of law, medicine, science, and education. Through such cooperation the Gospel gradually permeates the institutions of society, not through coercion, but through the faithful witness and disciplined collaboration of Christian communities.

Such renewal would involve stronger connections between

[22] Pope Pius XI, *Ubi Arcano Dei Consilio* (Vatican City: Vatican Press, A.D. 1922), §20.

parishes, schools, families, and Catholic professionals. It would encourage the creation of businesses, organizations, and cooperative ventures rooted in Catholic principles of justice, dignity, and solidarity. It would foster communities in which work, worship, and service reinforce one another rather than existing in separate spheres of life.

These efforts would not replace the Church's works of mercy. Rather, they would strengthen them. When communities are healthy, when work is dignified, when families are stable, and when moral principles shape economic life, fewer people fall into the desperation that requires emergency charity.

The Church in America already possesses the people, the institutions, and the tradition required for such renewal. What remains is the decision to act.

Sacred Scripture repeatedly calls believers to perseverance in the work entrusted to them: "Therefore, my beloved brethren, be ye steadfast and immovable: always abounding in the work of the Lord, knowing that your labour is not in vain in the Lord."[23]

The crisis of the modern age is not merely political or economic. It is spiritual and cultural. It concerns the very question of what kind of civilization we intend to build for the generations that follow us. Catholics

---

[23] The Holy Bible, Translated from the Latin Vulgate, Douay-Rheims Edition (Baltimore: John Murphy Company, A.D. 1899), 1 Corinthians 15:58.

cannot remain spectators in this struggle. If the faith is true, and the Church has always proclaimed that it is, then it must shape not only the private lives of believers but the structures of society itself.

Catholic Action is the recognition of that responsibility. It is the conviction that the future will not be secured simply by preserving fragments of the past. It must be built again.

This book therefore proposes a renewal of *Catholic Action in America*, not merely as charity, but as the deliberate rebuilding of Catholic institutions, Catholic economic life, and Catholic community in the twenty-first century.

The pages that follow outline a practical framework for renewing Catholic life across several areas of society. The project described here is ambitious, yet it remains grounded in institutions and traditions that already exist within the life of the Church. It is not intended as a rigid blueprint, but as a model that can be adapted according to the circumstances of each diocese, the resources available, and the talents of the faithful who undertake the work.

C. A. Chuba
Pittsburgh, Pennsylvania
March, A.D. 2026

CATHOLIC ACTION IN AMERICA

A Practical Manual for Building Diocesan Networks, Guilds, and Christian Institutions in the Twenty-First Century

Chapter I

The Diocese and Christian Civilization

The Roman and Apostolic Origins of the Diocese

✠ ✠ ✠

The structure through which the Church organizes her life is not accidental. From the earliest centuries of Christianity, the Church developed a territorial form of governance in which a defined community of believers was entrusted to the pastoral care of a bishop. This structure, known as the diocese, gradually became the ordinary framework through which Christian life was organized. Within it the Church administered the sacraments, cared for the poor, taught the faith, and maintained unity among the faithful.

The word itself has ancient origins. In the later Roman Empire, the term *diocese* referred to a large administrative district composed of several provinces. Roman authorities used these divisions to govern a vast and diverse empire by organizing authority according to territory rather than tribe, language, or profession. When Christianity spread throughout the empire, the Church adopted and transformed aspects of this administrative framework. The Church did not imitate the empire merely for convenience. Rather, she adapted the territorial logic of Roman governance to serve the pastoral mission entrusted to her by Christ.

From the beginning, the Christian community understood itself as a visible society ordered under shepherds appointed to guide the faithful. The Acts of the Apostles describes the early leaders of the Church as guardians of a particular flock. St. Paul instructed the elders of Ephesus in these words: "Take heed to yourselves, and to the whole flock, wherein the Holy Ghost hath placed you bishops, to rule the Church of God."[24]

This pastoral language reveals a central principle of Christian organization. The Church was never meant to exist as a loose association of believers scattered without structure. It was a community gathered around the teaching authority and sacramental ministry of its shepherds. As the Gospel spread from city to city, each Christian community developed under the leadership of a bishop who served as the visible sign of unity for that territory.

One of the earliest witnesses to this structure was St. Ignatius of Antioch in the first century. Writing to Christians throughout the Roman

---

[24] The Holy Bible, Translated from the Latin Vulgate, Douay-Rheims Edition (Baltimore: John Murphy Company, A.D. 1899), Acts 20:28.

world, he emphasized the importance of unity around the local bishop: "Where the bishop appears, there let the people be; just as wherever Jesus Christ is, there is the Catholic Church."[25]

This early testimony reveals how closely the life of the Christian community was tied to a particular place. The bishop was not merely a traveling teacher or distant administrator. He was the shepherd of a defined flock living within a specific city and its surrounding countryside. Around him gathered the clergy who assisted in the ministry of the Church and the faithful who shared in the sacramental life of the community.

As Christianity expanded beyond the cities into rural regions, this territorial structure gradually developed into the parish system. The word *parish* derives from the Greek *paroikia*, meaning a community dwelling together in a particular place. Priests were assigned to care for smaller local congregations while remaining united under the authority of the bishop of the diocese. In this way the life of the Church extended outward from the cathedral to the surrounding towns and villages.

The cathedral itself symbolized the center of this unity. The name comes from the *cathedra*, the chair of the bishop from which he teaches and governs the faithful entrusted to him. From this seat the bishop exercises the pastoral authority given to the apostles and transmitted through the

[25] St. Ignatius of Antioch, *Letter to the Smyrnaeans*. In *The Apostolic Fathers*. Translated by J. B. Lightfoot and J. R. Harmer (London: Macmillan, A.D. 1891), 8:2.

centuries in the sacrament of Holy Orders. The cathedral therefore stands not merely as an architectural monument but as the visible heart of diocesan life.

St. Cyprian of Carthage expressed this unity between bishop and community with remarkable clarity in the third century: "The Church is in the bishop and the bishop is in the Church; and if anyone is not with the bishop, he is not in the Church."[26]

Within this structure the early Christian community organized its common life. The bishop oversaw the administration of the sacraments, guarded the teaching of the faith, and ensured that charity was extended to those in need. Deacons and priests assisted in these responsibilities, while the faithful themselves participated actively in the life of the community through works of charity, mutual aid, and public witness to the faith.

The territorial organization of the Church proved remarkably stable. As the Roman Empire passed through periods of political turmoil and eventual decline in the West, the diocesan structure remained intact. Bishops continued to guide their communities even when imperial authority weakened or disappeared. In many regions the Church preserved learning, administered charity, and maintained social order during times when civil institutions were collapsing.

---

[26] St. Cyprian of Carthage, *Epistle 66*. In *The Ante-Nicene Fathers*, Volume 5 (Buffalo: Christian Literature Publishing Co., A.D. 1886), 8.3.

This durability was not accidental. The diocesan system provided a natural framework for organizing Christian life within a defined territory. It connected the sacramental ministry of the Church to the daily lives of the faithful. It allowed local communities to develop institutions of education, charity, and economic cooperation while remaining united to the universal Church through the authority of their bishop.

For this reason, the diocese became more than an administrative arrangement. It became the living foundation upon which Christian society was built. Within its boundaries the faithful worshiped together, cared for one another, educated their children, and organized the institutions that sustained their communities. Over time monasteries, confraternities, charitable associations, and professional guilds would grow within this territorial framework, forming the social fabric of Christian civilization.

This unity of the Christian community around the bishop was already clearly recognized in the earliest centuries of the Church. St. Ignatius of Antioch wrote to the Christians of Smyrna in these words: "See that you all follow the bishop, even as Jesus Christ follows the Father, and the presbytery as the apostles."[27]

These words express a principle that remained constant throughout the history of the Church. The diocese is not simply a bureaucratic district.

---

[27] St Ignatius of Antioch, *Letter to the Smyrnaeans*. In *The Apostolic Fathers*. Translated by J. B. Lightfoot and J. R. Harmer (London: Macmillan, A.D. 1891), 8:1.

It is a living community in which clergy and laity cooperate in the mission of the Church under the pastoral authority of the bishop.

In the centuries that followed, this territorial structure became the framework through which Christian civilization itself developed. Parishes, monasteries, schools, and charitable institutions grew within the boundaries of the diocese, shaping the cultural, social, and spiritual life of entire regions. Within this structure the Church did not merely preach the Gospel. She organized a way of life through which the faith could take root in communities and endure across generations.

The Diocese as the Structure of Christian Society

✠✠✠

The diocesan structure did more than organize the internal life of the Church. Over time it became the framework within which Christian society itself developed. Because the diocese united worship, authority, and community within a defined territory, it allowed the faith to shape not only individual souls but the social life of entire regions.

Christian life has always possessed a deeply local character. The faithful do not encounter the Church primarily through distant institutions or abstract ideas. They encounter it in a particular place, among particular people, within a community where the sacraments are celebrated and the faith is lived. The parish church, the cathedral, the monastery, and the charitable institutions of the diocese formed a network through which the spiritual and social life of Christians became intertwined.

The early Church recognized that the faith could not remain confined to private belief. The Gospel called believers to build communities ordered according to the law of charity. The Acts of the Apostles describes the life of the first Christians in language that reveals this communal character: "And all they that believed were together, and had all things common."[28]

This passage does not describe a political ideology but a way of life rooted in shared faith and mutual responsibility. Within the diocesan structure, Christians learned to order their common life around the needs of the community and the moral teachings of the Church.

As Christianity spread across Europe and the Mediterranean world, this territorial organization gradually gave rise to a rich network of institutions. Parishes became centers of daily life where the faithful gathered for worship, instruction, and mutual support. Monasteries preserved learning, cultivated land, and offered hospitality to travelers and the poor. Schools attached to cathedrals and monasteries educated new generations in both sacred and classical learning.

Alongside these religious institutions arose associations formed by

---

[28] The Holy Bible, Translated from the Latin Vulgate, Douay-Rheims Edition (Baltimore: John Murphy Company, A.D. 1899), Acts 2:44.

the laity themselves. Confraternities brought together believers who shared particular devotional practices or charitable works. Burial societies ensured that the poor received proper Christian funerals. Mutual aid associations provided support for widows, orphans, and members who fell into hardship.

One of the most important of these lay institutions was the guild. Guilds were associations of craftsmen, merchants, and professionals organized according to their trade. Each guild typically operated under the patronage of a particular saint and maintained a close relationship with the parish or cathedral of the city in which it operated. Members attended Mass together, supported charitable works, and upheld ethical standards within their profession.

Guilds did more than regulate economic activity. They helped shape the moral life of the community. Apprentices were trained not only in technical skill but also in Christian conduct. Masters were expected to treat their workers with justice. The guild itself often supported chapels, processions, and charitable institutions within the diocese.

In this way, economic life became closely connected to the religious life of the community. Work was not treated as a purely commercial activity detached from moral responsibility. It was understood as part of a broader vocation within Christian society. The Church taught that human labor participates in the creative work of God and must therefore be ordered toward the common good. St. Paul expressed this principle clearly in his letter to the Thessalonians: "For even when we were with you, this we declared to you: that if any man will not work, neither let him eat."[29]

This teaching did not glorify wealth or profit for their own sake. Rather it affirmed the dignity of productive work within the life of the community. Labor was meant to support families, sustain the poor, and contribute to the stability of society.

The diocesan structure allowed these institutions to function within a coherent moral framework. The bishop provided spiritual authority and doctrinal guidance, while lay associations carried out many of the practical activities that sustained daily life. Clergy and laity therefore worked together within a shared order that united worship, work, and charity.

The Christian tradition consistently taught that the goods of society exist not merely for private gain but for the benefit of the whole community. St. Basil the Great expressed this principle with striking clarity when he wrote: "The bread which you keep belongs to the hungry; the cloak which you store in your chest belongs to the naked."[30]

Christian society sought to realize this principle by organizing

---

[29] The Holy Bible, Translated from the Latin Vulgate, Douay-Rheims Edition (Baltimore: John Murphy Company, A.D. 1899), 2 Thessalonians 3:10.
[30] St. Basil the Great, *Homily on Avarice*. In *Nicene and Post-Nicene Fathers*, Second Series, Volume 8 (New York: Christian Literature Publishing Co., A.D. 1895), §7.

institutions that served both spiritual and temporal needs. The parish nurtured the sacramental life of the faithful. The guild ensured the dignity and stability of labor. The monastery cultivated learning and charity. Each of these institutions operated within the territorial unity of the diocese.

Because of this integration, the Church did not function as a separate religious sphere existing alongside society. The faith permeated the structures of daily life. Festivals, processions, and liturgical seasons shaped the rhythm of the year. Markets and workshops operated within communities guided by Christian moral teaching. Charity toward the poor was not left solely to the state but carried out through local institutions rooted in the life of the Church.

Over many centuries this network of dioceses, parishes, monasteries, and guilds formed the social fabric of Christian civilization. It allowed communities to sustain themselves spiritually, economically, and culturally within a shared moral order.

This system did not eliminate sin or injustice, but it provided a framework in which society could be guided by the teachings of the Church. The institutions of Christian life reinforced one another, and the faithful lived their daily lives within structures that reflected their religious convictions.

Yet this social order did not endure unchanged. Beginning in the later medieval and early modern period *(A.D. 1500-1800)*, a series of political, economic, and ideological transformations gradually weakened the institutions that had sustained Catholic civil society for centuries.

To understand the challenges facing the Church today, it is necessary to examine how that older system was dismantled and replaced by the structures of the modern secular world.

The Dissolution of Catholic Civil Society

✠ ✠ ✠

The system described in the previous sections did not disappear suddenly. For many centuries the institutions of Christian civilization remained remarkably stable. Parishes continued to anchor local communities, monasteries preserved learning and charity, and guilds regulated economic life according to principles shaped by the moral teaching of the Church. The diocese provided a structure through which these institutions could cooperate within a shared religious framework.

Yet beginning in the later medieval and early modern periods *(A.D. 1500–1800)*, this social order gradually weakened. Political upheaval, economic transformation, and religious conflict disrupted the institutions that had sustained Catholic civil society for centuries. What had once functioned as an integrated network of religious, social, and economic life slowly fragmented under the pressure of new forces.

The Diocese and Christian Civilization

One of the earliest turning points came with the consolidation of centralized monarchies and the growing power of secular states. In several regions of Europe rulers began to assert authority over institutions that had previously operated within the autonomy of the Church and local communities. Guilds and confraternities, which had long governed trades and professions, were increasingly viewed as obstacles to centralized economic control. Monastic lands and charitable foundations became tempting targets for rulers seeking new sources of wealth.

The upheavals of the Reformation accelerated this transformation. In countries where Catholic institutions were suppressed, vast networks of monasteries, guilds, and charitable foundations were confiscated or dismantled. One of the most dramatic examples occurred in England during the reign of Henry VIII and his successors *(A.D. 1536-1541)*. The dissolution of the monasteries in the sixteenth century destroyed hundreds of religious houses that had served as centers of charity, education, and agricultural stewardship. At the same time many guilds and confraternities lost their property and legal status.

These changes had consequences far beyond religious life. The monasteries had provided employment, charity, and economic stability across large regions of the country. Guilds had regulated wages, training, and standards of production within their trades. When these institutions disappeared, the social protections they offered disappeared with them.

The economic system that gradually emerged in their place was profoundly different from the older Catholic order. Instead of a network of locally governed guilds and associations, economic life increasingly became organized around large concentrations of capital and the expansion of wage labor. Land that had once supported monastic communities or small agricultural holdings was consolidated into larger estates or commercial enterprises.

The English Catholic writer Hilaire Belloc described this transformation with particular clarity in his analysis of modern economic history. In *The Servile State* he argued that the destruction of the medieval guild system created a society in which the majority of people no longer possessed productive property of their own. Instead they became dependent upon wages paid by those who controlled land and capital. As Belloc observed, "The control of the means of production is divorced from the mass of the citizens."[31] Over time this imbalance between ownership and labor produced a new form of social instability.

According to Belloc, the economic order that replaced the guild system was neither the free and widely distributed property ownership that earlier Catholic society had encouraged, nor the communal ownership later proposed by socialist movements. Instead, it concentrated productive

---

[31] Hilaire Belloc, *The Servile State* (London: T. N. Foulis, A.D. 1912). Chapter 2.

property in the hands of a relatively small class of owners while the majority of the population depended upon wage labor for survival.

This new economic structure came to be known as industrial capitalism. It was characterized by rapid technological development, large-scale manufacturing, and expanding markets that stretched far beyond local communities. While it produced immense economic growth in certain regions, it also disrupted the older social networks that had once connected work, family, and faith within the territorial life of the diocese.

As industrial capitalism spread across Europe and North America, many workers experienced harsh conditions and growing insecurity. The traditional institutions that had once provided mutual support were gone, and new industrial systems often placed profit above the well-being of communities. Writing in the nineteenth century, Pope Leo XIII described the conditions of the industrial working class in stark terms: "A small number of very rich men have been able to lay upon the teeming masses of the laboring poor a yoke little better than that of slavery itself."[32]

These conditions eventually gave rise to a powerful reaction.

In the nineteenth century socialist and communist movements emerged as critics of industrial capitalism. These movements recognized the deep social inequalities created by the concentration of property and capital.

[32] Pope Leo XIII, *Rerum Novarum* (Vatican City: Vatican Press, A.D. 1891), §3.

Yet their proposed solutions rejected many of the moral and religious foundations that had once guided Christian society. Rather than restoring the network of local institutions that had characterized Catholic civilization, many socialist movements sought to transfer economic power to centralized states that would manage production on behalf of society.

The result was a long conflict between two systems that appeared to oppose one another but shared a common origin. Both capitalism and communism developed within a secular framework that had already severed economic life from the religious and social institutions of the Church. One system concentrated power in private economic structures while the other concentrated it in the state. Neither restored the integrated local order that had once existed within Christian civilization. As Pope Pius XI later warned, "Religious socialism, Christian socialism, are contradictory terms; no one can be at the same time a sincere Catholic and a true socialist."[33]

---

33 Pope Pius XI, *Quadragesimo Anno* (Vatican City: Vatican Press, A.D. 1931), §120.

Chapter II

The Crisis of the Catholic Laity

The Forgotten Role of the Catholic Laity

✠ ✠ ✠

The structure of Christian civilization described in the previous chapter did not arise solely from the work of clergy. Bishops, priests, and religious orders played essential roles in guiding the spiritual life of the Church, but the daily institutions of society were largely built and sustained by the laity themselves. Farmers cultivated the land, craftsmen produced the goods necessary for daily life, merchants organized trade, and professionals governed civic institutions. Within this network of work and responsibility, lay Catholics shaped the practical structures of Christian society.

From the earliest centuries of the Church, the faithful understood that the life of the Christian community extended far beyond the walls of the church building. The Gospel called believers not only to worship God but also to order their daily lives according to the principles of charity, justice, and mutual responsibility. In this way, the faith shaped the institutions of family life, economic activity, and local governance.

Sacred Scripture repeatedly reminds believers that the Christian vocation encompasses every aspect of life. St. Paul wrote to the Colossians: "All whatsoever you do in word or in work, do all in the name of the Lord Jesus Christ, giving thanks to God and the Father by him."[34]

Within this body the clergy are entrusted with particular responsibilities. Bishops and priests administer the sacraments, teach the faith, and guard the unity of the Church. Yet the work of shaping society belongs in large measure to the laity, whose daily occupations place them within the economic and social life of the community. Their vocation is not secondary to the mission of the Church but essential to it.

The Catechism of the Catholic Church expresses this principle clearly: "The lay faithful are called to seek the kingdom of God by engaging in temporal affairs and by ordering them according to the plan of God."[35]

For many centuries this understanding guided the participation of lay Catholics in public life. The faithful did not imagine the Church as an institution confined to worship alone. They built schools, hospitals, charitable foundations, and professional associations that reflected the

34 The Holy Bible, Translated from the Latin Vulgate, Douay-Rheims Edition (Baltimore: John Murphy Company, A.D. 1899), Colossians 3:17.

35 Catechism of the Catholic Church (Vatican City: Libreria Editrice Vaticana, A.D. 1992), §898.

moral teaching of the faith. Guilds regulated economic life, confraternities organized works of devotion and charity, and local civic institutions were often led by men whose formation had taken place within the life of the Church.

In medieval and early modern Europe the social fabric of many towns and cities depended heavily upon these lay institutions. Guilds trained apprentices and upheld ethical standards within their trades. Confraternities cared for the sick, buried the dead, and provided assistance to families in distress. Lay patrons financed churches, hospitals, and schools that served the wider community.

The clergy provided spiritual leadership and doctrinal guidance, but the practical work of building society was carried out largely by the faithful who lived and labored within the world. In this sense, Christian civilization was never merely a clerical enterprise. It was a partnership between spiritual authority and lay initiative, each operating within its proper sphere.

St. John Chrysostom reminded Christians that faith must extend beyond the sanctuary into the ordinary responsibilities of life. Reflecting on the duties of believers within society, he wrote: "The Christian must not imagine that religion concerns only prayer and worship; it must also shape the conduct of daily life."[36]

---

[36] St. John Chrysostom, *Homilies on the Gospel of Matthew*. In *Nicene and Post-Nicene Fathers*, First Series, Volume 10 (New York: Christian Literature Publishing Co., A.D. 1888), Homily 5.

Over time, however, this partnership weakened. The gradual disappearance of guilds, confraternities, and other Catholic associations removed many of the structures through which the laity had once exercised their social responsibility. As these institutions faded, the participation of many Catholics in organized Catholic life became increasingly limited to the sacramental and devotional activities of the parish.

The result has been a narrowing of the Catholic imagination. For many believers the Church now appears primarily as a place one attends rather than a society in which one participates. The parish remains an essential center of worship and sacramental life, but it often lacks the network of lay institutions that once connected faith with daily economic and social activity.

This reduction of Catholic life to passive participation has profound consequences. When the laity no longer organize institutions rooted in the moral teaching of the Church, the structures that govern daily life are formed by other forces. Economic systems, cultural industries, and political institutions increasingly develop according to principles that do not reflect the Christian understanding of the human person.

The Church continues to proclaim the Gospel and administer the sacraments, yet the surrounding social order often operates according to a different vision of human life. In such circumstances the faithful may find themselves living in societies shaped by values that contradict the teachings they profess.

This situation does not arise from a failure of faith alone. It also reflects the disappearance of the institutional structures through which lay Catholics once exercised their responsibilities within society. Without organized cooperation among the faithful, individual believers remain isolated within systems that they did not create and do not control.

For this reason the renewal of Catholic life in the modern world cannot depend solely upon increased religious devotion. Devotion remains essential, but it must be accompanied by the rebuilding of the institutions through which the laity participate in the social mission of the Church.

The question that therefore arises is not whether lay Catholics should participate in the life of the Church. That participation is already assumed. The deeper question concerns how the faithful can once again organize their talents, professions, and resources in ways that allow the moral vision of Christianity to shape the structures of society.

Only when the laity recover this sense of responsibility will the Church once again possess the social vitality that once characterized Christian civilization. The renewal of Catholic culture will depend not only upon the fidelity of clergy but also upon the initiative of believers who bring the principles of the faith into the institutions of daily life.

The Separation of Church and State Problem

✠ ✠ ✠

The weakening of lay Catholic institutions did not occur in isolation. It developed alongside a broader transformation in the political and intellectual life of the modern world. Over several centuries, Western societies gradually moved away from the older understanding that religion formed the moral foundation of public life. In its place emerged a new political doctrine which claimed that religion should remain confined to the private sphere of individual belief.

This change is often described in modern language as the "Separation of Church and State." In its original and limited sense, the phrase referred to the distinction between spiritual authority and civil governance. The Church has long recognized this distinction. Christ Himself acknowledged the existence of legitimate civil authority when He declared: "Render therefore to Caesar the things that are Caesar's; and to God the things that are God's."[37]

Yet the older Christian understanding of this distinction did not imply that religion should be excluded from public life. Rather it recognized that civil authority and spiritual authority possess different responsibilities within the same moral order. The Church guided the spiritual life of the

[37] The Holy Bible, Translated from the Latin Vulgate, Douay-Rheims Edition (Baltimore: John Murphy Company, A.D. 1899), Matthew 22:21.

faithful and taught the moral law, while political authority governed the temporal affairs of society.

For many centuries, Christian rulers and institutions operated within this shared framework. Laws, customs, and public institutions were shaped by moral principles that drew heavily from the teachings of the Church. Religious festivals structured the calendar, Christian charity informed social policy, and public life assumed the existence of a moral law grounded in divine authority.

The modern concept of separation gradually altered this relationship. Beginning in the early modern period, many political thinkers proposed that religion should be treated as a purely private matter. The state would govern society according to principles derived from human reason alone, while religious belief would be left to the conscience of individuals.

At first this shift appeared to promise peace within societies divided by religious conflict. Yet over time it produced a deeper transformation. If religion was confined to the private life of individuals, then the institutions that organized society would inevitably be shaped by principles other than the moral teaching of the Church.

Pope Leo XIII later warned that such a division between religion and public life would eventually weaken the moral foundations of society itself. Reflecting on the political consequences of this separation, he wrote:

"It would be a grave error to hold that the Church ought to be separated from the State, and the State from the Church."[38]

The consequences of this shift were far-reaching. Economic systems developed without reference to Christian social teaching. Political ideologies emerged that treated religion as irrelevant or even harmful to public life. Educational institutions gradually removed religious instruction from their curricula. In many countries the moral language that had once guided law and public debate was replaced by purely secular concepts of rights, power, and individual autonomy.

This transformation did not eliminate religion entirely, but it changed its role within society. Faith became increasingly understood as a personal preference rather than a public foundation for social order. Religious communities continued to worship and teach their members, yet the institutions that governed economic, political, and cultural life often developed independently of those teachings.

The Catechism of the Catholic Church recognizes the importance of religious freedom while also affirming that human societies must acknowledge the moral law revealed by God: "The duty of offering God genuine worship concerns man both individually and socially."[39]

This teaching reflects a fundamental principle of Catholic thought.

---

38 Pope Leo XIII, *Immortale Dei* (Vatican City: Vatican Press, A.D. 1885), §6.
39 Catechism of the Catholic Church (Vatican City: Libreria Editrice Vaticana, A.D. 1992), §2105.

Human beings are not merely private individuals who happen to hold religious beliefs. They are members of communities whose laws, institutions, and customs inevitably reflect some vision of the human person and the moral order.

When religion is excluded from public life, another vision inevitably takes its place. In modern societies that vision is often shaped by secular ideologies that treat individual autonomy or economic power as the highest principles of social organization.

For Catholics the consequences of this transformation are especially significant. If religion is confined to private devotion, the institutions that shape daily life will be formed according to values that may differ sharply from the teachings of the Church. Schools, businesses, cultural institutions, and political systems may operate according to principles that do not reflect the Christian understanding of human dignity, family life, or the common good.

The result is a growing tension between the faith professed by believers and the structures within which they live and work. Catholics may gather in their parishes for worship, yet their professional and social lives unfold within institutions shaped by entirely different assumptions about morality and human purpose.

This situation creates a subtle but powerful pressure. When religious belief is treated as a private matter, the faithful may gradually come to accept that their faith has little relevance for the organization of society. The Church remains present as a place of worship and spiritual consolation, but the broader structures of culture and economy develop according to other principles.

Over time this division weakens the ability of Catholic communities to sustain a distinct cultural identity. Families raise their children within the faith, yet those children grow into a society whose institutions operate according to values that often contradict the moral teachings they received.

The challenge facing the Church in the modern world therefore extends beyond individual belief. It concerns the relationship between faith and the social structures that shape daily life. If Catholics wish to preserve and transmit their moral tradition, they must find ways to organize their communities so that the institutions surrounding them reinforce rather than undermine the teachings of the Church.

The Return of Catholic Action

✠ ✠ ✠

If the weakening of Catholic civil society has been accompanied by the decline of organized lay institutions, the renewal of Christian civilization must necessarily involve their restoration. The Church has never taught that the laity exists merely as spectators within the life of the faith. Rather, the faithful are called to bring the principles of the Gospel into the daily structures of society through their work, their professions, and their civic responsibilities.

Sacred Scripture repeatedly emphasizes the responsibility of believers to shape the world around them according to the law of God. Christ Himself used the image of leaven within bread to describe the quiet but transformative influence of the faithful within society: "The kingdom of heaven is like to leaven, which a woman took and hid in three measures of meal, until the whole was leavened."[40]

The image is instructive. Leaven is a small portion of fermented dough or yeast that spreads through a much larger mass of dough and causes it to rise. It does not exist apart from the dough but works slowly from within until the whole loaf is transformed. In the same way the Christian vocation is not fulfilled only within acts of private devotion. The faithful are called to influence the structures of daily life through the institutions they build and the communities they form.

This responsibility became especially clear during the social upheavals of the nineteenth century. Industrialization had transformed economic life, large urban populations had replaced older village communities, and secular political movements were reshaping the laws and

---

[40] The Holy Bible, Translated from the Latin Vulgate, Douay-Rheims Edition (Baltimore: John Murphy Company, A.D. 1899), Matthew 13:33.

institutions of many nations. Catholic leaders increasingly recognized that the renewal of Christian society could not be accomplished by clergy alone. It required the organized cooperation of the laity.

One of the most influential expressions of this effort came through the development of Catholic social teaching. In A.D. 1891 Pope Leo XIII issued the encyclical *Rerum Novarum*, which addressed the conditions created by industrial capitalism and the rise of socialist movements. The document encouraged Catholics to form associations capable of protecting workers, strengthening families, and promoting the common good within modern economic life.

Building upon this foundation, Catholic leaders throughout Europe began to organize lay movements dedicated to applying Christian principles within society. Workers' associations, youth organizations, professional groups, and charitable networks emerged with the support of bishops and clergy. These initiatives sought not only to defend the rights of Catholics but also to shape the broader moral culture of society.

Within this context the term *Catholic Action* gradually came to describe the coordinated participation of the laity in the apostolic mission of the Church. Pope Pius XI strongly encouraged this organized lay apostolate, writing: "The faithful, and especially the laity, should take a more active part in the apostolate of the Church."[41]

This teaching clarified an important principle. The clergy possess the authority to teach, sanctify, and govern within the Church. The laity, however, possess direct influence within the ordinary structures of society. They work in fields, factories, schools, businesses, hospitals, courts, and political institutions. Through these occupations they shape the daily life of their communities.

If those professions are organized according to Christian principles, they strengthen the moral life of society. If they are not, the institutions that govern daily life will inevitably reflect other values.

St. Francis de Sales expressed this same idea when he reminded Christians that holiness must be lived within the ordinary duties of daily life. Writing in the seventeenth century, he observed: "It is an error, or rather a heresy, to wish to banish the devout life from the army, from the workshop, from the court, or from the household."[42]

The purpose of *Catholic Action* is precisely to ensure that the Christian life remains present within these ordinary spheres of society. It does not replace the sacramental life of the Church, nor does it compete with the authority of the clergy. Rather, it extends the moral and social influence of the Church through the organized work of the faithful.

---

[41] Pope Pius XI, *Ubi Arcano Dei Consilio* (Vatican City: Vatican Press, A.D. 1922), §13.
[42] St. Francis de Sales, *Introduction to the Devout Life* (Annecy: Chez J. Jullieron, A.D. 1609), Part I, Chapter 3.

Catholic Action in America

Historically this effort often took the form of associations, guilds, mutual aid societies, professional organizations, and charitable institutions. These groups allowed Catholics to cooperate with one another in economic life, education, and social service while remaining united to the moral teaching of the Church.

Such organizations strengthened both the faith and the stability of local communities. They allowed Catholics to support one another in their professions, assist families in moments of need, and transmit their cultural and religious traditions across generations.

The disappearance of many of these institutions in the modern era has left Catholic communities increasingly dependent upon social structures that do not reflect the moral teaching of the Church. Without organized cooperation among the faithful, individual believers often find themselves isolated within systems that operate according to entirely different principles.

The renewal of *Catholic Action* therefore requires more than personal devotion. It requires the rebuilding of the networks through which the laity cooperate in shaping society itself.

The diocese provides the natural framework for this effort. Under the pastoral leadership of the bishop, Catholic professionals, workers, educators, and families can organize associations that strengthen the social and economic life of the Christian community. Through such cooperation the talents and resources of the faithful can once again serve the mission of the Church within the broader structures of society.

The chapters that follow explore how this renewal might take practical form within the life of a diocese. They examine the ways in which Catholic institutions, professions, and communities could once again cooperate so that the moral vision of the Gospel informs the structures of social life.

Chapter III

The Structure of Catholic Action

The Catholic Action Executive Council

✠ ✠ ✠

If Catholic life is to be renewed within the diocese, cooperation among the faithful cannot remain informal or scattered. Institutions do not arise merely from goodwill or enthusiasm. They require structure, discipline, and leadership capable of coordinating the many talents that exist within the Christian community.

The Church herself has always recognized the necessity of ordered authority. From the earliest centuries the faithful gathered around the bishop as the visible shepherd of the local Church. Within the diocese the bishop remains the guardian of doctrine, the overseer of the sacraments, and the spiritual father of the Christian community. This unity reflects not only a practical arrangement but a deeper theological reality. As Sacred

Scripture teaches: "Obey your prelates, and be subject to them. For they watch as being to render an account of your souls."[43]

Yet the practical work of organizing the social and economic life of the faithful must be carried out largely by the laity themselves. Their professions, skills, and daily occupations place them within the institutions that shape society. For this reason, any serious effort to rebuild Catholic civil society requires a body capable of coordinating the work of lay associations under the guidance of the Church.

The *Catholic Action Executive Council* is proposed as such a body. It serves as the coordinating leadership structure through which Catholic professionals, guilds, and charitable associations can organize their work in cooperation with the pastoral authority of the bishop. Its purpose is not to create a parallel hierarchy within the Church, but to provide an instrument through which the laity may carry out their social responsibilities in an orderly and disciplined manner.

At the head of the Executive Council stands a president chosen from among respected members of the Catholic community. The president is responsible for guiding the overall direction of *Catholic Action* within the diocese, coordinating the efforts of its various institutions, and ensuring unity among the different sectors of Catholic life.

---

[43] The Holy Bible, Translated from the Latin Vulgate, Douay-Rheims Edition (Baltimore: John Murphy Company, A.D. 1899), Hebrews 13:17.

Supporting this role is a vice president who assists in administration and strategic coordination. The vice president ensures continuity of leadership and is prepared to assume the responsibilities of the president and other council roles in the event of absence or vacancy. In this way stability is preserved, and the work of the council is not disrupted by changes in leadership.

Alongside this lay leadership stands a chaplain appointed in consultation with diocesan authority. The chaplain serves as the spiritual anchor of the Executive Council, ensuring that its work remains firmly rooted in the moral teaching and sacramental life of the Church. His presence safeguards the unity between practical action and spiritual authority, so that *Catholic Action* remains an extension of the Church's mission rather than a merely secular enterprise.

Because *Catholic Action* involves the cooperation of many different sectors of society, accountability within the organization is essential. For this reason, the Executive Council includes three auditors, each representing one of the principal chambers through which Catholic life is organized: the *Chamber of Collegiate Guilds*, the *Chamber of Labor Guilds*, and the *Chamber of Charitable Associations.*

Each auditor is responsible for overseeing the integrity and effectiveness of the institutions within his respective chamber. He ensures that financial practices remain transparent, that organizational conduct reflects the moral teaching of the Church, and that the activities of each chamber contribute to the broader mission of *Catholic Action*. Through this structure the diverse work of the faithful is brought into unity without losing the distinct character of each vocation.

The council is further supported by an executive secretary responsible for the practical administration of the organization. Through the work of administrative secretaries, communication between parishes, guilds, charitable institutions, and the broader Catholic community is maintained with clarity and efficiency. The stability of any large organization depends upon such disciplined administration, without which even well-ordered plans can falter.

A particularly important role within this structure is that of the steward of diocesan lands and physical resources, the warden. Throughout Christian history the stability of communities has depended in part upon the wise management of material goods. Churches, schools, farms, and charitable institutions require physical space in which to operate. The careful stewardship of these resources ensures that the work of *Catholic Action* is not only spiritually grounded but materially sustainable.

The Executive Council does not attempt to govern every activity directly. Rather, it provides the structure through which the many associations of Catholic life can act in concert. As St. Basil the Great observed in his reflections on communal life: "Nothing is so characteristic of a well-ordered community as that each member contributes to the common good according to his ability."[44]

Such coordination allows the diverse talents of the faithful to be united within a shared purpose.

The importance of disciplined leadership cannot be overstated. Institutions often fail not because their aims are misguided but because their organization is weak. When authority is unclear or responsibilities are poorly defined, even generous efforts dissipate without lasting effect. As Sacred Scripture reminds us: "For where there is no governor, the people shall fall."[45]

Taken together, these offices form the governing structure of the *Catholic Action Executive Council.* The president provides direction and unity of purpose, while the vice president ensures continuity and stability in leadership. The chaplain maintains the spiritual integrity of the council's work, grounding all activity in the life and teaching of the Church. The three auditors, each assigned to one of the principal chambers of Catholic society, uphold accountability and order within their respective spheres. The warden of diocesan lands ensures the proper stewardship of the material resources upon which Catholic institutions depend, while the

---

[44] St. Basil the Great, *The Longer Rules.* In *Ascetical Works* (New York: Fathers of the Church, A.D. 1950), q. 7.
[45] The Holy Bible, Douay-Rheims Edition (Baltimore: John Murphy Company, A.D. 1899), Proverbs 11:14.

executive secretary sustains the administrative coordination necessary for the council's operation. In their unity, these roles constitute the *Catholic Action Executive Council*, a body ordered toward the disciplined and faithful renewal of Catholic life within the diocese.

The Three Chambers of Catholic Society

✠ ✠ ✠

A society cannot endure without a structure that allows its various forms of work to operate in harmony. Different vocations contribute distinct goods to the life of the community. Some govern and teach, others build and produce, and others care for those in need. When these forms of activity are rightly ordered, they sustain both the material and moral life of society.

Christian civilization historically organized these forms of work through a network of guilds and associations. These institutions did more than regulate economic activity. They formed communities of responsibility. They trained individuals in their craft, upheld standards of conduct, and ensured that work served not only private interest but the common good. In this way economic life was integrated into a broader moral and social order.

Although the formal guild system has largely disappeared, the underlying reality has not. Human work still gathers people into natural communities. Professionals, laborers, and charitable workers each operate within distinct spheres that shape the life of society. What is often lacking in the modern world is not cooperation itself, but a unifying moral framework that orders these spheres toward a common end.

For this reason *Catholic Action* proposes that the work of the faithful within the diocese be organized into three principal chambers. These chambers correspond to the fundamental ways in which society is sustained: the formation of institutions and knowledge, the production of material goods, and the care of the vulnerable.

The first is the *Chamber of Collegiate Guilds*. This chamber gathers those professions that shape the intellectual, legal, and institutional life of society. Lawyers, physicians, educators, engineers, financial professionals, and scholars all belong to this sphere. Their work carries particular weight because it influences the structures through which society is governed and understood.

The Christian tradition has long recognized that knowledge must be ordered toward truth and charity. St. Augustine warned that learning detached from love becomes destructive rather than beneficial: "Knowledge puffs up, but charity edifies."[46]

For this reason the work of professionals cannot remain morally

---

[46] St. Augustine, *De Doctrina Christiana (On Christian Doctrine)*. Translated by J. F. Shaw (Edinburgh: T. & T. Clark, A.D. 1873), Book I, Chapter 36.

neutral. When guided by Christian principles, these vocations strengthen justice and truth. When separated from them, they risk constructing systems that obscure both.

The second is the *Chamber of Labor Guilds.* This chamber gathers those whose work sustains the material life of the community. Farmers cultivate food, builders construct homes, craftsmen produce goods, and tradesmen maintain the systems upon which daily life depends. These vocations provide the physical foundation without which no society can endure.

The dignity of such labor has always been affirmed within the Christian tradition. St. Benedict, whose rule shaped much of Western civilization, united work and spiritual life in a single discipline: "They are truly monks when they live by the labor of their hands."[47]

This insight extends beyond the monastery. Human labor is not merely economic activity. It is a disciplined participation in the ordering of life itself. The organization of labor guilds within *Catholic Action* restores this vision by recognizing that those who build and produce are essential to the stability of the community.

The third is the *Chamber of Charitable Associations.* This chamber coordinates the works of mercy carried out by Catholic institutions and the

[47] St. Benedict of Nursia, *The Rule of St. Benedict.* Translated by Rev. Boniface Verheyen (London: Burns & Oates, A.D. 1875), Chapter 48.

faithful. From the earliest centuries, the care of the poor, the sick, and the vulnerable has stood at the center of Christian life. These works are not optional expressions of generosity but necessary expressions of justice and love.

St. John Chrysostom spoke with particular clarity about this responsibility, reminding Christians that charity is not separate from faith but a direct expression of it: "If you cannot find Christ in the beggar at the church door, you will not find Him in the chalice."[48]

For this reason, charitable work must be organized, not left to isolated acts of goodwill. By gathering these institutions within a unified chamber, *Catholic Action* strengthens cooperation among the many works already present within the diocese. Resources, knowledge, and personnel can be shared in a way that increases both effectiveness and stability.

Taken together, these three chambers represent the principal forms of activity that sustain a healthy society. The Collegiate Guilds shape institutions and knowledge. The Labor Guilds provide the material foundation of life. The Charitable Associations ensure that the weak are not abandoned.

When these spheres operate independently, society becomes fragmented. Intellectual life drifts away from moral truth, economic activity

---

[48] St. John Chrysostom, *Homilies on the Gospel of Matthew*. In *Nicene and Post-Nicene Fathers*, First Series, Volume 10 (New York: Christian Literature Publishing Co., A.D. 1888), Homily 50.

becomes detached from human dignity, and charitable efforts struggle without the support of broader social structures. When they are united within a common framework, however, they reinforce one another. Knowledge serves truth, labor sustains community, and charity restores what has been wounded.

The chamber system therefore provides a practical method for organizing Catholic society according to vocation while maintaining unity across the whole. Each chamber retains its proper function, yet all are ordered toward a shared purpose under the coordination of the Executive Council.

Through this structure, the faithful are able not only to share resources, personnel, and knowledge, but to place their collective capacities at the service of the diocese itself. When work must be undertaken, whether in education, construction, legal matters, or charitable care, the Church need not look outward to distant or indifferent institutions. She may draw instead from within her own community, calling upon the organized talents of her people to carry out the necessary tasks with fidelity and purpose. In this way the diverse forms of work within the diocese remain not only coordinated, but actively united in the service of a common mission.

The Role of Boards

✠ ✠ ✠

If the chambers provide the broad organization of Catholic society according to vocation, the boards provide the means by which that society acts. A community may possess skilled professionals, dedicated laborers, and charitable institutions, yet without defined instruments of coordination, their efforts remain dispersed. The boards therefore exist as the operational structures through which the work of *Catholic Action* is directed toward concrete ends within the life of the diocese.

Each board draws its members from the relevant guilds and associations, ensuring that its decisions are informed by real expertise rather than abstract theory. At the same time, each board operates under the authority of the Executive Council, preserving unity of purpose across the wider structure of *Catholic Action.* In this way, knowledge is not isolated and authority is not fragmented. Instead, the various forms of competence within the community are brought into ordered cooperation.

The Legal and Arbitration Board serves as the foundation of justice within this system. By drafting standardized contracts, advising Catholic institutions, and operating internal tribunals for dispute resolution, it provides a stable framework within which economic and social life can function. Its work reflects a principle long recognized in Christian tradition, that justice must be ordered, impartial, and rooted in truth. St. Augustine observed that peace itself depends upon right order, writing, "Peace is the tranquillity of order."[49] Without such order, even well-intentioned communities can fall into conflict or confusion. The presence of a coherent legal structure therefore protects both individuals and institutions while reinforcing the unity of the whole.

Closely connected to this is the work of the Economic Development Board, which directs the material resources of the diocese toward long-term stability and growth. By coordinating credit systems, investment funds, land stewardship, and business development, it ensures that economic life remains oriented toward the common good rather than short-term gain. The Church has consistently taught that economic activity must serve the dignity of the human person and the needs of the community. St. John Chrysostom warned against the misuse of wealth in stark terms: "Not to share one's goods with the poor is to rob them and deprive them of life."[50] The Economic Development Board therefore does not pursue wealth as an end in itself, but as a means of sustaining families, supporting institutions, and strengthening the independence of Catholic communities.

---

[49] St. Augustine, *De Civitate Dei (City of God)*. Translated by Marcus Dods (New York: Random House, A.D. 1950), Book XIX, Chapter 13.
[50] St. John Chrysostom, *Homily on Lazarus and the Rich Man*. In *Nicene and Post-Nicene Fathers*, First Series, Volume 9 (New York: Christian Literature Publishing Co., A.D. 1889), Homily 2.

The Education Board turns to a different but equally essential task: the formation of the next generation. No society can endure if it fails to transmit its intellectual, moral, and cultural inheritance. By coordinating schools, apprenticeships, homeschooling support, and vocational training, this board ensures that education is not reduced to technical instruction alone. Rather, it becomes the formation of the whole person within a Christian understanding of truth. The Catechism affirms this responsibility with clarity: "Parents have the first responsibility for the education of their children."[51] The work of the Education Board extends this formation into the wider life of the community, ensuring that learning remains rooted in faith, culture, and discipline.

The Healthcare Board addresses the physical and psychological well-being of the community. Drawing from the Medical Guild, it coordinates care in a manner that respects both human dignity and Catholic moral teaching. Its work includes the development of cooperative healthcare systems, support for the vulnerable, and preparation for times of crisis. In this it reflects the long tradition of Christian care for the sick, which has always been understood as a direct expression of charity. From the earliest hospitals founded by the Church, care for the suffering has been

---

[51] Catechism of the Catholic Church (Vatican City: Libreria Editrice Vaticana, A.D. 1992), §2223.

treated not as an optional service but as a necessary work of mercy embedded within the life of the community.

The Security and Infrastructure Board fulfills a role that is often overlooked but indispensable. No community can flourish without stability and protection. By organizing physical security, cybersecurity, emergency preparedness, and infrastructure resilience, this board safeguards the conditions necessary for all other forms of activity. Its work preserves not only property and systems, but the freedom of the Church to carry out her mission without disruption. In times of crisis, the presence of an organized and disciplined response ensures that communities remain intact rather than dissolving under pressure.

Alongside this stands the Benedictus Certification Board, which establishes moral and economic standards for participation in the Catholic economy. Through certification, oversight, and public accountability, it ensures that businesses operating within the diocesan network adhere to principles of just wages, ethical sourcing, and responsible stewardship. This function restores a key element of the older guild system, in which economic activity was judged not only by efficiency but by moral integrity. By creating recognizable standards, the Benedictus Board strengthens trust and encourages Catholics to support institutions that reflect their shared moral commitments.

The Youth and Family Development Board addresses the most fundamental unit of society: the family. Through mentorship programs, formation initiatives, and support for marriage and parenting, it seeks to strengthen the relationships upon which all other institutions depend. The stability of families determines the stability of communities. Without deliberate formation, the transmission of faith and culture weakens over time. This board ensures that young people are not left to navigate modern society without guidance, but are formed within networks of responsibility, discipline, and shared purpose.

Finally, the Sacred Arts and Cultural Life Board restores the dimension of beauty within Catholic society. A civilization is not sustained by economics and governance alone. It is expressed through art, music, literature, and shared celebration. By supporting sacred music, visual arts, festivals, and cultural institutions, this board ensures that the life of the Church remains not only functional but expressive of the beauty of the faith. What is believed must also be seen, heard, and celebrated if it is to endure across generations.

Taken together, these boards provide the means by which *Catholic Action* becomes concrete. They translate principles into institutions and intention into sustained activity. Each board operates within its own sphere, yet all remain united under the Executive Council and ordered toward the life of the diocese as a whole.

The Structure of Catholic Action

Through this structure, the Church regains something that has largely been lost in the modern world: the ability to act as a coordinated society. Legal systems, economic development, education, healthcare, security, family life, and culture are no longer left to external forces alone. They are shaped, in part, by the organized efforts of the faithful themselves.

In this way the boards do not merely administer functions. They restore the practical capacity of Catholic society to order its common life according to the principles of the Gospel.

Chapter IV

The Organization of the Diocesan Commonwealth

Identifying Catholic Personnel

✠ ✠ ✠

The renewal of Catholic society within a diocese does not begin with buildings, financial capital, or administrative programs. It begins with people. Every institution, whether a school, a charitable association, or an economic enterprise, depends upon the skill, character, and cooperation of those who sustain it. Before structures can be built, the persons capable of sustaining them must be recognized.

For this reason, the first practical step in rebuilding Catholic civil society is the identification of the human resources already present within the life of the Church. In every parish there exist individuals whose talents quietly uphold the daily functioning of society. Among the faithful are physicians, farmers, engineers, teachers, carpenters, accountants, attorneys, craftsmen, and artists. These are not incidental members of the Church. They are the very means through which Christian life can take visible and institutional form within the world.

The Christian tradition has always understood that such talents are not merely personal possessions. They are entrusted gifts ordered toward service. St. Irenaeus expressed this vision with characteristic clarity when he wrote, "The glory of God is man fully alive."[52] Human capacity finds its fulfillment not in isolation, but in participation in the life of the community and in service to the purposes of God.

When these capacities remain scattered, their potential is diminished. Individuals work, produce, and contribute within separate systems, often without awareness of one another. When they are brought into relationship, however, a new possibility emerges. The physician, the builder, the teacher, and the merchant cease to function merely as isolated professionals. They become collaborators in the construction of a common life.

Modern society organizes professional activity through networks that are largely secular in character. Lawyers gather in legal associations, physicians in medical boards, and entrepreneurs in commercial systems that

---

[52] St. Irenaeus of Lyons, *Adversus Haereses (Against Heresies)*. In *The Ante-Nicene Fathers*, Volume 1 (Buffalo: Christian Literature Publishing Co., A.D. 1885), Book IV, Chapter 20, Section 7.

operate according to principles often detached from the moral vision of the Church. These structures provide coordination, but they rarely provide direction. They enable cooperation, but not necessarily toward the good that the Christian tradition understands as the fulfillment of human life.

For this reason, *Catholic Action* begins not by replacing these structures, but by recognizing and ordering the human capacities already present within the Church. A practical means of accomplishing this is the creation of a comprehensive directory of Catholic professionals and tradesmen within the diocese. Parish communities can identify the occupations and skills of their members, forming a clear picture of the talents available within the Catholic population.

Such a directory functions as more than a record. It becomes a form of self-knowledge for the community. The Church comes to see not only who her members are, but what they are capable of building together. In this sense, the identification of personnel is the first act of reconstruction. It reveals that the resources necessary for renewal are not entirely external. They already exist within the body of the faithful.

This insight corresponds to a deeper theological principle. The Church is not merely an assembly of individuals. She is a living organism ordered toward a common end. St. Thomas Aquinas observed that "each individual is related to the whole community as part to whole."[53] When the talents of the faithful are united, they participate in a higher form of order than any one person could achieve independently.

Once these capacities are identified, they can be directed toward the formation of guilds and associations. Experienced professionals can be called upon to guide and mentor younger members of the community, establishing a continuity of knowledge and practice across generations. In this way, professional formation becomes inseparable from moral formation.

St. Gregory the Great emphasized the responsibility inherent in such leadership, writing, "No one does more harm in the Church than he who has the title or rank of holiness and acts perversely."[54] The formation of future generations therefore requires not only technical instruction but the example of integrity. Mentorship becomes a transmission not only of skill, but of character.

Through this process, a gradual transformation begins to take place. Work is no longer understood merely as private employment. It is seen as participation in a shared vocation. The farmer, the craftsman, the physician, and the teacher each contribute to the stability and flourishing of

---

[53] St. Thomas Aquinas, *Summa Theologiae*. Translated by the Fathers of the English Dominican Province (New York: Benziger Brothers, A.D. 1947), II–II, q. 58, a. 5.
[54] St. Gregory the Great, *Pastoral Rule*. Translated by Henry Davis (London: Burns & Oates, A.D. 1950), Book I, Chapter 2.

the community. Their labor becomes intelligible within a larger moral and spiritual framework.

The identification of Catholic personnel is therefore not a preliminary administrative step. It is the foundation upon which the entire structure of *Catholic Action* rests. Without it, plans remain theoretical. With it, the Church begins to recover the capacity to act as an organized society.

Once the human resources of the community have been identified, the next step is to connect them through systems of communication capable of sustaining cooperation across the entire diocese. The tools required for this task are readily available in the modern world, but their effective use depends upon clarity of purpose and fidelity to the principles that guide the work.

Technology and Communication Infrastructure

✠ ✠ ✠

Once the talents and professions of the Catholic community have been identified, the next task is to ensure that these individuals and institutions remain connected to one another. A society cannot function without reliable channels of communication. Knowledge, requests for assistance, opportunities for cooperation, and awareness of need must circulate through a network that allows people to act together rather than in isolation. Without such connection, even the most capable community remains fragmented.

Throughout her history, the Church has always depended upon systems of communication to preserve unity across distance. The apostolic age itself was sustained through correspondence, as bishops and missionaries maintained communion among scattered communities. In later centuries, monasteries preserved and transmitted knowledge through disciplined labor, while the rhythms of parish life were marked by visible and audible signs that gathered the faithful into a common life. These were not merely practical tools. They were instruments of unity.

Modern technology introduces new means for accomplishing the same purpose. Digital communication, when rightly ordered, allows a diocese to function not as a collection of isolated parishes, but as a coherent society. It enables cooperation across distance, strengthens relationships between institutions, and allows the faithful to respond quickly to both opportunity and need. Technology, in this sense, becomes not an end in itself, but a servant of communion.

The first step in establishing such a system is the creation of a diocesan communication platform capable of integrating the various elements of *Catholic Action.* This may take the form of a central digital hub supported by secure internal systems connecting guilds, boards, and parish communities. Through such a platform, members of the faithful can identify available services, locate professionals, and participate in projects that serve the wider diocesan mission.

The importance of unity in communication has been emphasized since the earliest days of the Church. St. Ignatius of Antioch, writing to the Christians of Ephesus, urged them to remain united not only in belief but in action: "Let there be one prayer, one supplication, one mind, one hope in love."[55] Communication within the diocesan network must serve precisely this end. It is not merely the exchange of information, but the preservation of unity in purpose.

Beyond basic communication, digital infrastructure can provide concrete tools that sustain cooperation. Directories allow members of the faithful to identify Catholic professionals and institutions. Parishes can coordinate volunteers and events. Guilds can organize projects that require multiple trades or areas of expertise. In this way, communication becomes the framework within which action becomes possible.

These systems also strengthen professional collaboration. Engineers may share technical knowledge, educators may develop and exchange curriculum, and medical professionals may coordinate care and resources. What once required proximity can now be sustained across the entire territory of the diocese. The result is a network that mirrors, in a modern form, the interconnected life of earlier Christian societies.

---

[55] St. Ignatius of Antioch, *Letter to the Ephesians*. In *The Apostolic Fathers*. Translated by J. B. Lightfoot and J. R. Harmer (London: Macmillan, A.D. 1891), Chapter 4.

At the same time, the use of such technology requires discipline. Communication that is rapid but careless can damage trust rather than strengthen it. For this reason, digital systems must be guided not only by efficiency, but by truth and responsibility. St. Francis de Sales, reflecting on the moral use of speech, taught that "truth which is not charitable proceeds from a charity which is not true."[56] The same principle applies to modern communication. Information must be reliable, measured, and ordered toward the good of the community.

Security likewise becomes essential. As communication increasingly takes place through digital systems, the protection of personal data, institutional records, and financial activity must be ensured. The integrity of the network depends upon the trust of those who use it. Without proper safeguards, the very tools designed to unite the community may expose it to harm or exploitation.

The Church has also recognized that communication carries a responsibility toward the common good. The Catechism teaches that "information provided by the media must be in the service of the common good."[57] Within the diocesan network, this principle takes on a concrete form. Communication must strengthen cooperation, promote clarity, and

---

[56] St. Francis de Sales, *Introduction to the Devout Life*. Translated by John K. Ryan (New York: Doubleday, A.D. 1955), Part III, Chapter 29.
[57] Catechism of the Catholic Church (Vatican City: Libreria Editrice Vaticana, A.D. 1992), §2494.

support the mission of the Church rather than distract from it.

When such systems function well, they transform the daily life of the faithful. A builder can quickly locate skilled collaborators. A family in need can be connected with charitable assistance. A Catholic business can find both workers and customers within the community. The faithful begin to perceive not only the needs around them, but their own ability to respond.

St. Basil the Great described the Christian community as one in which no member lives for himself alone, but for the good of all: "The bread which you keep belongs to the hungry; the cloak which you store in your chest belongs to the naked; the shoes rotting in your house belong to the barefoot."[58] This vision becomes tangible when communication allows individuals to recognize one another and act together. The network does not create the community. It reveals it and enables it to function.

Technology, therefore, does not replace the personal and sacramental life of the Church. It supports it. It provides the means by which a dispersed population becomes a coordinated society. Properly ordered, it allows the Church to act with clarity, speed, and unity in a world that is increasingly shaped by complex systems of information and communication.

---

[58] St. Basil the Great, *Homily on Avarice (Homily to the Rich)*. In *Nicene and Post-Nicene Fathers*, Second Series, Volume 8 (New York: Christian Literature Publishing Co., A.D. 1895), §7.

Once the human resources of the Catholic community have been identified and connected through reliable communication systems, attention must turn to another foundation of stability: the physical resources of the diocese. Land, buildings, and material assets provide the space within which institutions operate, and their proper stewardship will determine the long-term strength of Catholic society.

Mapping Land and Physical Resources

✠ ✠ ✠

Human communities cannot endure without a material foundation. Families require homes, institutions require buildings, and economic life requires land upon which work can be carried out. For this reason, any serious effort to rebuild Catholic social life must take into account not only people and communication, but the physical resources that sustain them.

Throughout Christian history, the stability of Catholic institutions has depended upon the careful stewardship of land and property. Monasteries cultivated fields that fed surrounding populations. Parishes maintained schools, halls, and houses of charity. Hospitals and hospices arose not as abstractions, but as concrete places in which the works of mercy were carried out. These resources were never regarded merely as financial assets. They were instruments placed at the service of the Christian community.

The first step in recovering this vision is a comprehensive survey of the land and buildings already entrusted to the diocese. Many dioceses possess a wide range of properties, including parish grounds, schools, retreat centers, cemeteries, rectories, farmland, and facilities that have fallen into disuse. Yet these assets are often managed individually rather than understood as parts of a unified whole.

A careful mapping of these resources allows the Church to see her material foundation clearly. Parish properties can be catalogued, unused structures identified, and land suitable for development evaluated in light of future needs. What emerges from such an effort is not merely a list of holdings, but a vision of possibility. The diocese begins to recognize what it is capable of sustaining through its own resources.

The Christian understanding of land has always been shaped by the principle of stewardship. The earth is not ultimately owned in an absolute sense, but entrusted to human care. As St. Ambrose taught, "The earth was established for all, not for the rich alone."[59] This teaching reminds the faithful that material resources carry a social dimension. They are given not only for private use, but for the good of the community.

Once diocesan properties have been identified, the next task is to discern how they may serve the long-term development of Catholic life.

---

[59] St. Ambrose, *De Nabuthe Jezraelita (On Naboth)*. In *Nicene and Post-Nicene Fathers*, Second Series, Volume 10 (New York: Christian Literature Publishing Co., A.D. 1896), Chapter 12.

Some lands may be suited for agriculture, contributing to food stability and local economic resilience. Others may provide opportunities for housing that allows families to live near parishes and schools. Still others may be dedicated to education, charity, or cultural life.

Such decisions require prudence. The needs of each diocese differ according to geography, population, and existing institutions. In some regions, farmland may be essential. In others, the priority may be the preservation of schools or the development of community centers. By considering these resources together, rather than in isolation, the Church can begin to act with foresight rather than reaction.

This approach reflects a broader principle found within the tradition. St. Thomas Aquinas teaches that the use of material goods must be ordered toward the needs of others, observing that "in cases of necessity all things are common property."[60] Property, therefore, is not an absolute possession detached from moral responsibility. It is part of a larger order directed toward human flourishing.

To assist in this work, modern technology can again be employed in a constructive way. The creation of an ***interactive diocesan resource map*** allows the faithful to visualize the physical infrastructure of their community. Churches, schools, charitable institutions, farmland, and other

---

[60] St. Thomas Aquinas, *Summa Theologiae*. Translated by the Fathers of the English Dominican Province (New York: Benziger Brothers, A.D. 1947), II–II, q. 66, a. 7.

properties can be seen not as isolated locations, but as interconnected elements of a single system.

Such a map also reveals what is often hidden. Underutilized buildings can be identified and repurposed. Vacant land can be directed toward productive use. Facilities that once served earlier generations can be renewed to meet present needs. In this way, the past is not discarded, but integrated into the future development of the Church.

The long-term goal of this work is not simply efficient management, but stability. A community that possesses and wisely governs its physical resources is less dependent upon external systems and less vulnerable to sudden disruption. It is capable of sustaining its institutions across generations.

St. John Chrysostom expressed this responsibility in terms that extend beyond almsgiving to the entire use of material goods, teaching, "The rich man is not one who is in possession of much, but one who gives much."[61] This insight reveals that the value of material resources lies not in their accumulation, but in their proper use. Land, buildings, and property fulfill their purpose when they sustain families, support institutions, and contribute to the stability of the community. When they are left idle or used without regard for the common good, they cease to serve the ends for

[61] St. John Chrysostom, *Homily on First Timothy*. In *Nicene and Post-Nicene Fathers*, First Series, Volume 13 (New York: Christian Literature Publishing Co., A.D. 1889), Homily 12.

which they were entrusted.

By mapping both the human and physical resources of the diocese, *Catholic Action* establishes the conditions necessary for renewal. The talents of the faithful, the systems that connect them, and the land that sustains their work together form the infrastructure of a functioning Christian society.

Chapter V

Catholic Education and the Formation of a People

The Failure of Industrial Education

✠ ✠ ✠

No civilization can endure unless it succeeds in forming the minds and character of the next generation. Education determines not only what a society knows, but what it loves, what it remembers, and what it considers worthy of honor. For this reason, the structure of education is never neutral. It shapes the soul of a people.

For many centuries, Christian education was ordered toward the formation of the whole person. Schools attached to monasteries, cathedrals, and parishes sought to cultivate wisdom, discipline, and clarity of thought. Students were introduced to Sacred Scripture, classical literature, philosophy, theology, music, and the practical arts that sustained daily life. Learning was not conceived as mere preparation for employment, but as preparation for participation in a civilization ordered toward God.

St. Jerome, reflecting on the formation of the young, warned that education must begin with what is lasting rather than what is fleeting, writing, "Let her be trained in such studies as will make her a good Christian."[62] Education, in this sense, is not simply the accumulation of knowledge, but the shaping of the soul according to truth.

This older vision stands in sharp contrast to the model that now dominates much of modern education. The prevailing system in America, which developed under the influence of the nineteenth-century Prussian state, was designed to produce disciplined workers and obedient citizens for an industrial and bureaucratic order. Its purpose was not the cultivation of wisdom, but the formation of efficiency, uniformity, and compliance.

Within this model, students are organized by age into standardized grades, subjects are divided into isolated compartments, and progress is measured through examinations and numerical performance. The structure mirrors the logic of the factory and the administrative state. Time is segmented, tasks are assigned, and results are evaluated according to external metrics. The student is gradually formed not as a free and virtuous person, but as a participant in a system.

Such a model cannot serve as the foundation of Catholic

---

[62] St. Jerome, *Letter 107 to Laeta*. In *Nicene and Post-Nicene Fathers*, Second Series, Volume 6 (New York: Christian Literature Publishing Co., A.D. 1893), §4.

education. A system designed to produce factory workers and soldiers cannot be the instrument through which a Christian people is formed. It may produce competence, but it cannot produce wisdom. It may train the mind, but it does not necessarily order the soul.

The consequences of this shift are visible in the lives of many students who pass through modern educational systems. After years of schooling, they often possess fragments of specialized knowledge but lack a coherent understanding of their own intellectual and spiritual inheritance. They may be fluent in the language of contemporary culture while remaining unfamiliar with the traditions that gave rise to the civilization in which they live.

St. Augustine described this disorder with remarkable insight, observing that education without proper orientation leads not to wisdom but to confusion: "They are learned in many things, but they know not themselves."[63] Knowledge, when detached from truth and self-understanding, fragments rather than unifies.

This fragmentation is intensified by the surrounding culture of distraction. Modern students are immersed in a constant stream of entertainment, information, and digital stimulation. Their attention is drawn toward what is immediate and novel, while what is enduring and formative

[63] St. Augustine, *Confessions*. Translated by E. B. Pusey (London: John Henry Parker, A.D. 1838), Book X, Chapter 8.

is often neglected. The result is an imagination shaped more by passing trends than by permanent truths.

The effects extend beyond intellectual formation into cultural memory. A generation may emerge that can navigate digital systems with ease yet cannot identify the historical, geographical, and spiritual foundations of its own society. Such a condition is not merely an educational failure. It is a civilizational risk. A people that loses its memory loses its identity.

The Church has consistently taught that education must aim at the full development of the human person. This includes not only intellectual formation, but moral discipline, cultural inheritance, and the capacity to exercise freedom responsibly. St. John Bosco, who dedicated his life to the education of the young, expressed this mission simply: "Education is a matter of the heart."[64] Formation requires not only instruction, but relationship, discipline, and love.

The industrial model of education, by contrast, tends to reduce learning to measurable performance. It prepares students for participation in economic systems while often neglecting the deeper question of how they ought to live. It equips them with skills, but not always with judgment. It provides information, but not necessarily wisdom.

---

[64] St. John Bosco, *Letter from Rome*. In *The Biographical Memoirs of St. John Bosco*. Translated by Diego Borgatello (New Rochelle: Salesiana Publishers, A.D. 1984), A.D. 1884 Letter.

This reduction has profound consequences for the understanding of vocation. In the Christian tradition, vocation refers to a calling, a participation in the order of creation directed toward the good. Work is not merely a means of survival or advancement. It is a form of service within a larger moral and social order.

Modern education rarely speaks in such terms. Students are encouraged to pursue careers based on opportunity or preference, often without reference to the common good or the moral meaning of their work. The language of vocation is replaced by the language of utility and self-enrichment.

Yet society cannot be sustained by utility alone. It requires individuals who understand their place within a larger order and who are capable of acting with wisdom and responsibility. Education must therefore do more than prepare students for employment. It must prepare them for life within a community shaped by truth, justice, and charity.

For this reason, the renewal of Catholic education cannot consist merely in minor reforms to existing systems. It requires a recovery of the original purpose of education itself. Schools must once again become places where the intellect is formed, the will is disciplined, and the imagination is shaped by what is true and beautiful.

Only within such a vision can a people be formed who are capable of sustaining a Christian civilization.

Classical Education and Cultural Formation

✠ ✠ ✠

If the industrial model of education has narrowed the purpose of learning, the recovery of a classical Christian approach offers a path toward restoring the deeper formation of the human person. Classical education does not treat knowledge as information to be accumulated. It seeks to cultivate wisdom, judgment, and the intellectual habits necessary for responsible participation in society.

The Christian tradition did not reject the intellectual inheritance of the ancient world. It received it, purified it, and elevated it. Early Christian scholars preserved the works of Greek and Roman authors while placing them within a moral framework illuminated by revelation. In this way, the study of language, philosophy, literature, and theology became the foundation of an education ordered not merely toward competence, but toward understanding.

At the center of this tradition stood a fundamental conviction. Truth can be known, and the human intellect is capable of discovering it through disciplined inquiry. Yet this pursuit was never separated from the formation of character. Knowledge was meant to guide action. It was meant to illuminate the path of human life within a moral order established by God.

St. Bonaventure expressed this unity of knowledge and its divine source with precision, writing, "All knowledge is a kind of illumination, and every illumination is from God."[65] Learning, therefore, is not an autonomous human achievement. It is a participation in a greater light that gives coherence to all things.

Within this vision, students were introduced to the great works that shaped Western civilization. They encountered classical authors, the writings of the Church Fathers, the poetry and history of earlier ages, and the theological reflections that gave structure to Christian thought. Through such study, the mind was trained not merely to absorb information, but to discern meaning, to recognize order, and to judge rightly.

Language played a decisive role in this formation. The study of Latin, and often Greek, allowed students to encounter texts in their original form. These languages were not simply academic exercises. They were the living threads that connected generations across centuries. Through them, students entered into a conversation that extended beyond their own time.

This linguistic training also disciplined the mind. Grammar required precision. Logic cultivated coherence. Rhetoric formed the ability to speak truth with clarity and persuasion. Together, these disciplines shaped what medieval educators recognized as the foundation of intellectual life.

---

[65] St. Bonaventure, *Itinerarium Mentis in Deum (The Journey of the Mind to God).* Translated by Philotheus Boehner (Indianapolis: Hackett Publishing Company, A.D. 1993), Prologue.

Catholic Education and the Formation of a People

St. Isidore of Seville, reflecting on the purpose of learning, wrote, "Unless you know what has been written before, you cannot know what ought to be written now."[66] Education, in this sense, is inseparable from memory. It depends upon an inheritance received and understood.

For this reason, classical education is not only intellectual formation. It is cultural formation. Civilizations endure because they remember. Literature, history, and philosophy preserve the accumulated wisdom of a people. Through them, each generation receives not only knowledge, but identity.

When this memory is lost, societies become unstable. Individuals may possess technical skill, yet lack the historical awareness necessary to guide its use. They may be informed about the present moment, yet unable to interpret it within a larger context. Without memory, judgment becomes shallow, and decision becomes reactive.

The Christian tradition has always understood remembrance as a moral act. To remember is to remain rooted in truth. To forget is to become vulnerable to confusion. St. John Henry Newman observed that "to be deep in history is to cease to be Protestant."[67] His point extends more broadly. Depth in history anchors the mind. It protects against the

---

[66] St. Isidore of Seville, *Etymologiae*. Translated by Stephen A. Barney (Cambridge: Cambridge University Press, A.D. 2006), Book I.
[67] St. John Henry Newman, *An Essay on the Development of Christian Doctrine* (London: James Toovey, A.D. 1845), Introduction.

fragmentation that comes from living only in the present.

Through the study of history, literature, and philosophy, students begin to perceive themselves as participants in a larger story. They are not isolated individuals pursuing private advancement. They are heirs to a civilization that carries both achievements and responsibilities. This awareness forms the foundation of genuine citizenship.

Such formation also prepares individuals for leadership. A society requires men and women capable of judgment, capable of recognizing the consequences of their decisions across time. Leaders without historical and cultural awareness often govern poorly because they lack the ability to see beyond immediate circumstances.

Classical education seeks to cultivate precisely this depth. By engaging the great questions of philosophy, theology, and history, it trains the mind to think in terms of causes, consequences, and principles. It forms individuals who are capable of acting with prudence rather than impulse.

The goal is not antiquarianism.[68] It is not the preservation of the past for its own sake. It is the formation of persons capable of sustaining a just and ordered society. The knowledge of earlier ages becomes a guide for present action and a foundation for future development.

Yet intellectual formation alone is not sufficient. A stable society

---

[68] ***Antiquarianism***: the study and preservation of the past for its own sake, treating historical knowledge as an object of interest rather than as a guide for present action or future formation.

requires not only wisdom, but competence in the practical arts that sustain daily life. For this reason, classical education must be complemented by systems of apprenticeship and vocational training that connect learning with production, discipline, and service.

St. Benedict, whose rule shaped the educational and cultural life of Europe for centuries, united contemplation and labor in a single vision of human life. His principle remains instructive: "Let them prefer nothing whatever to Christ."[69] Even work itself must be ordered toward a higher end.

The final section of this chapter therefore turns to the recovery of apprenticeship and guild formation, through which intellectual and practical education may once again be united within a coherent and life-giving system.

Apprenticeship and Vocational Training

✠ ✠ ✠

While classical education forms the intellect and preserves the cultural memory of a civilization, a healthy society must also ensure that practical skills are transmitted across generations. Human communities depend not only upon scholars and teachers, but upon farmers, craftsmen, engineers, builders, and countless others whose work sustains daily life. For

---

[69] St. Benedict of Nursia, *The Rule of St. Benedict*. Translated by Rev. Boniface Verheyen (London: Burns & Oates, A.D. 1875), Chapter 72.

this reason, education must ultimately unite intellectual formation with the realities of productive work.

For much of Christian history, this unity was preserved through systems of apprenticeship. Young men and women learned their trades under the guidance of experienced masters who transmitted not only technical skill but discipline, responsibility, and a sense of purpose. The workshop, the farm, and the marketplace were not merely places of production. They were places of formation, where knowledge was acquired through participation in real work.

This approach reflected a distinctly Christian understanding of labor. Work was never regarded merely as a means of survival or profit. It was understood as a participation in the order of creation itself. St. John Chrysostom, reflecting on the dignity of ordinary labor, observed, "God has given us hands that we might work, not only for ourselves, but for others."[70] Labor, therefore, is inherently social. It binds individuals together within a network of mutual service.

Within the medieval world, this vision took institutional form in the guild system. Apprentices entered trades at a young age and advanced gradually under the supervision of masters. They learned not only how to perform their craft, but how to live within it. Standards of quality, honesty,

---

[70] St. John Chrysostom, *Homily on Acts*. In *Nicene and Post-Nicene Fathers*, First Series, Volume 11 (New York: Christian Literature Publishing Co., A.D. 1889), Homily 20.

and responsibility were upheld not by external regulation alone, but by the shared moral expectations of the community.

St. Joseph, though often silent in the Gospel, stands as a profound witness to this tradition. The Son of God Himself was formed within the household of a craftsman. St. Bernard of Clairvaux reflected on this mystery with reverence, noting that Christ "did not disdain to learn the trade of a carpenter."[71] In this simple fact, the dignity of labor is elevated beyond mere necessity. Work becomes a place of formation, even for the Incarnate Word.

The fruits of this tradition remain visible. Across Europe and the Americas stand churches, cathedrals, and civic buildings constructed by generations of craftsmen whose work united technical mastery with a profound sense of beauty. These structures were not designed merely to function. They were designed to endure, to elevate the mind, and to reflect the order of creation itself.

Yet many of these works now stand in quiet contrast to the systems that surround them. Modern society inherits the products of a civilization of craftsmen, while increasingly lacking the craftsmen themselves. Buildings are admired, but the skills required to create them are no longer widely cultivated. Beauty is preserved, but not reproduced.

---

[71] St. Bernard of Clairvaux, *Homily on the Missus Est*. In *Sermons on the Blessed Virgin Mary*. Translated by a Priest of Mount Melleray (Dublin: Browne and Nolan, A.D. 1920), Homily 2.

This loss is not accidental. It reflects a shift in the philosophy of education. When schooling is organized primarily around abstraction, standardization, and credentialing, the cultivation of practical skill becomes secondary. Craft is replaced by process. Art is replaced by efficiency. The formation of the hand is neglected in favor of the management of systems.

The result is not only economic, but cultural. A society that ceases to form craftsmen gradually loses its ability to produce beauty. Its structures become temporary, its work becomes utilitarian, and its environment reflects function rather than meaning.

St. Thomas Aquinas defined art as "right reason about things to be made."[72] Craft, therefore, is not merely mechanical activity, but the application of reason to material reality, shaping it according to order and purpose. When rightly ordered, it produces not only utility, but harmony, proportion, and beauty.

A renewed system of apprenticeship offers a path toward recovering this vision. Through the guild structures described in earlier chapters, experienced craftsmen and professionals can once again guide younger members of the community. Knowledge is transmitted not through abstraction alone, but through example, repetition, and discipline.

Such mentorship also strengthens the bonds of the community.

---

[72] St. Thomas Aquinas, *Summa Theologiae*. Translated by the Fathers of the English Dominican Province (New York: Benziger Brothers, A.D. 1947), I–II, q. 57, a. 3.

Young workers learn not only how to perform a task, but how to carry themselves within their vocation. They observe how faith informs work, how decisions are made, and how responsibility is carried. Formation becomes personal rather than impersonal, relational rather than institutional.

This approach also supports the stability of family life. When young men and women can see a clear path from education to meaningful work, they are better prepared to establish households and contribute to the economic life of their communities. Vocational clarity reduces uncertainty and strengthens the foundations upon which families are built.

The Christian tradition has long understood that work forms the person who performs it. St. John Paul II expressed this insight with clarity, writing that "man becomes more a human being through work."[73] Labor is not only something one does. It is something through which one is formed.

For this reason, education must prepare the young not only to think, but to do. It must unite contemplation with action, intellect with skill, and knowledge with responsibility. A society that fails to transmit these capacities will gradually lose the ability to sustain its own institutions.

By integrating classical education with apprenticeship and vocational formation, Catholic society can recover a more complete vision

---

73 Pope St. John Paul II, *Laborem Exercens* (Vatican City: Vatican Press, A.D. 1981), §9.

of human development. Students learn to think clearly, to understand their inheritance, and to apply their knowledge through work that serves the common good.

The renewal of Catholic civilization therefore depends not only upon ideas, but upon the formation of men and women capable of embodying them. The guilds, associations, and institutions described throughout this work will require individuals whose education has prepared them both for wisdom and for craft, for leadership and for service.

Chapter VI

Guilds and the Restoration of Vocational Society

The History and Purpose of Guilds

✠ ✠ ✠

Throughout much of Christian history, the organization of economic life did not revolve around vast corporations or anonymous market systems. Instead, it was structured through communities of craftsmen and professionals known as guilds. These institutions formed one of the most stable pillars of medieval and early modern society, uniting economic activity with moral responsibility, professional standards, and the welfare of the community.

A guild was not simply a trade association in the modern sense. It was a moral and social body rooted in the Christian understanding of work. Members shared a common craft, whether as masons, carpenters, bakers, physicians, or merchants. Together they established standards for training, quality, and conduct. These standards were not ordered merely toward efficiency or profit, but toward justice, stability, and the dignity of labor.

The Christian tradition understands work as part of a moral order that must be governed by reason and justice. St. Thomas Aquinas, reflecting on economic life, taught that "it is unlawful to take advantage of a man's necessity in order to sell him a thing for more than its worth."[74] Work, in this sense, is not confined to economic necessity or private gain. It is ordered toward justice, service, and the good of the community, and must be carried out in a way that reflects the moral law.

For this reason, the guilds of Christian Europe were closely connected to the religious life of their communities. Many were placed under the patronage of a saint and maintained a visible presence within the parish. Members attended Mass together, supported liturgical celebrations, and participated in works of charity. Worship and work were not separated into distinct spheres. They belonged to a unified vision of life.

St. Francis de Sales expressed this integration with clarity when he wrote that "devotion must be practiced in different ways by the gentleman, by the artisan, and by the servant."[75] Holiness does not remove a man from his work. It orders his work toward God.

---

[74] St. Thomas Aquinas, *Summa Theologiae*. Translated by the Fathers of the English Dominican Province (New York: Benziger Brothers, A.D. 1947), II–II, q. 77, a. 1.
[75] St. Francis de Sales, *Introduction to the Devout Life*. Translated by John K. Ryan (New York: Doubleday, A.D. 1955), Part I, Chapter 3.

Guilds also served as guardians of ethical order within economic life. Because craftsmen operated within a recognized community, their work was subject to the judgment of their peers. Standards were upheld through relationships of accountability. Dishonest practices damaged not only the individual, but the entire body to which he belonged.

St. Ambrose warned that injustice in economic life is never isolated, writing that "no one can enrich himself by injustice without impoverishing another."[76] Commerce, therefore, must remain subject to moral law. Skill alone is not sufficient. Justice must guide it.

At the center of the guild system stood apprenticeship. Young workers entered into long term relationships with masters who formed them not only in technique, but in discipline, patience, and responsibility. Knowledge was transmitted through imitation, correction, and repetition. It was learned through doing.

This form of formation shaped the whole person. The apprentice did not merely acquire a skill. He learned how to live within his vocation. He observed how work was carried out, how obligations were fulfilled, and how conduct reflected moral principles. Character and competence developed together.

Guilds also functioned as systems of mutual aid. When members

---

[76] St. Ambrose, *De Officiis Ministrorum.* In *Nicene and Post-Nicene Fathers,* Second Series, Volume 10 (New York: Christian Literature Publishing Co., A.D. 1896), Book I, Chapter 30.

suffered illness, injury, or financial hardship, the community responded. Widows were supported, orphans cared for, and the dead buried with dignity. Economic life was inseparable from the duty of charity.

St. Gregory the Great taught that love must take visible form in action, writing that "the proof of love is in the works."[77] The guild gave this principle institutional expression. Charity was not left to chance. It was built into the structure of the community itself.

For this reason, guilds became pillars of Christian civilization. They united labor with virtue, production with justice, and economic life with the spiritual life of the Church. The craftsman was not an isolated individual competing within an impersonal system. He belonged to a community ordered toward the common good.

The decline of these institutions marked a profound shift. As economic life became more centralized and impersonal, the bonds that once connected work to moral formation weakened. Production expanded, but responsibility became diffuse. Efficiency increased, but community diminished.

Yet the principles that sustained the guild system remain necessary. Human beings still require formation, accountability, and cooperation within their work. A society that neglects these needs may produce wealth,

---

[77] St. Gregory the Great, *Homilies on the Gospels*. In *Nicene and Post-Nicene Fathers*, Second Series, Volume 12 (New York: Christian Literature Publishing Co., A.D. 1895), Homily 30.

but it will struggle to sustain a stable moral and social order.

The renewal of vocational communities is therefore not an exercise in nostalgia. It is the recovery of something enduring. The guilds proposed here are not replicas of medieval institutions, but modern expressions of their essential principles. They provide a structure through which Catholics may once again unite their professional lives with the moral vision of the Church.

In this way, work is restored to its proper place. It becomes not merely a means of survival or advancement, but a vocation ordered toward service, excellence, and the common good.

The consequences of abandoning this vision are visible in the very landscapes that surround us. Much of the modern built environment reflects not the pursuit of beauty or permanence, but the logic of mass efficiency and profit margins. Buildings are designed to be constructed quickly, at minimal cost, and with little regard for durability or form. Materials are selected for affordability rather than endurance. Craftsmanship is replaced by process, and design is reduced to function alone.

It is therefore no surprise that many modern towns and cities possess a certain impermanence. Structures often deteriorate within a single generation, sometimes within the very lifetime of those who built them. Neighborhoods lose coherence, public spaces lack identity, and the built environment no longer reflects a shared vision of the good.

In contrast, earlier generations built with an awareness that their work would outlast them. Churches, civic buildings, and even ordinary homes were constructed with care, proportion, and a sense of responsibility to the future. The difference is not merely technological. It is moral and cultural.

In many respects, we no longer live among the works of a civilization confident in its purpose, but among the remnants of systems driven by efficiency alone. We inhabit, in a real sense, the ruins of mass production and short-term calculation, structures conceived without permanence and therefore unable to sustain it.

A restored culture of craftsmanship would not simply improve the appearance of our cities. It would recover a deeper principle, that human work should create what is lasting, meaningful, and worthy of the community it serves. Only when labor is once again ordered toward these ends can the built environment reflect the dignity of the people who inhabit it.

The Collegiate Guilds

✠ ✠ ✠

If the guild system is to be restored within modern Catholic society, it must include not only craftsmen and laborers but also the professions whose work governs the intellectual, technical, and administrative structures of modern life. Lawyers, physicians, engineers, educators, financial professionals, and communications specialists shape the institutions through which society operates. Their decisions influence law, healthcare, education, finance, and the transmission of knowledge itself. For this reason, the renewal of Catholic civil society requires the organization of these professions within what may be called the Collegiate Guilds.

Historically, the learned professions were never understood as merely commercial occupations. They were vocations entrusted with particular responsibilities toward the common good. The physician was a guardian of life, the lawyer a servant of justice, the teacher a steward of truth. Their authority was grounded not only in expertise, but in the moral obligations attached to that expertise.

St. Gregory Nazianzen warned that knowledge without moral formation becomes dangerous, writing, "It is not the possession of knowledge that is harmful, but its misuse."[78] Intellectual power, when detached from truth, does not elevate society. It destabilizes it.

In the modern world, however, many of these professions operate within vast and impersonal systems whose guiding principles are often divorced from the moral tradition that once shaped them. Legal systems are

---

[78] St. Gregory Nazianzen, *Orations*. In *Nicene and Post-Nicene Fathers*, Second Series, Volume 7 (New York: Christian Literature Publishing Co., A.D. 1894), Oration 2.

frequently reduced to procedural mechanisms without reference to natural law. Medical practice is often governed by bureaucratic and financial pressures that obscure the dignity of the human person. Financial systems move capital at enormous scale while remaining largely indifferent to the moral consequences of their decisions.

A further development has intensified this condition. Increasingly, professional judgment is being supplemented, and in some cases replaced, by automated systems, algorithmic decision-making, and artificial intelligence. These tools can process information with remarkable speed and efficiency, yet they do not possess judgment in the full human sense. They cannot weigh moral responsibility, interpret intention, or exercise prudence in complex and uncertain situations.

St. Thomas Aquinas teaches that prudence is not merely the accumulation of data, but "right reason applied to action."[79] This form of reasoning requires more than calculation. It requires moral vision, experience, and the ability to judge particular circumstances in light of the good.

For this reason, no system of automation can fully replace the role of the human professional. A physician must discern not only symptoms but the dignity of the patient. A lawyer must interpret not only statutes but

[79] St. Thomas Aquinas, *Summa Theologiae*. Translated by the Fathers of the English Dominican Province (New York: Benziger Brothers, A.D. 1947), II–II, q. 47, a. 2.

justice itself. A financial professional must consider not only returns but consequences. These are acts of judgment, not computation.

The increasing reliance on algorithmic systems therefore introduces a new risk. When decision-making is delegated entirely to processes that lack moral awareness, responsibility becomes obscured. Errors may be amplified, and unjust outcomes may be produced without clear accountability. In such a system, even the professional himself may become passive, deferring judgment rather than exercising it.

For this reason, the restoration of professional communities is even more urgent. Catholic professionals must not only preserve ethical standards within their fields, but also ensure that the tools they use remain subject to human judgment. Technology must assist, not replace, the exercise of reason. It must be examined, corrected, and governed by those who understand both its capabilities and its limits.

The Collegiate Guilds exist to overcome this isolation. They gather Catholic professionals into communities of shared discipline, shared knowledge, and shared moral commitment. Within the *Chamber of Collegiate Guilds*, each profession forms its own guild. Lawyers organize within a Legal Guild, physicians within a Medical Guild, educators within an Educators Guild, and so forth across the various professions represented within the diocese.

These guilds provide a structure through which professionals can consult one another, establish ethical standards, and support members who face moral challenges within their fields. A physician confronting difficult questions at the beginning or end of life, a lawyer navigating conflicts between legal practice and moral truth, or a financial professional evaluating the social consequences of investment decisions should not be left to act alone. Within the guild, such questions are examined within a shared framework of faith and reason.

This form of association reflects a principle affirmed within the Church's social teaching. Pope Leo XIII taught that "to enter into a society of this kind is the natural right of man; and the State must protect natural rights, not destroy them."[80] When individuals unite around a shared vision of the good, their work becomes more than individual effort. It becomes coordinated action ordered toward justice.

St. Hildegard of Bingen, reflecting on the harmony of knowledge and divine purpose, wrote that "all the arts serve the divine wisdom."[81] When rightly ordered, intellectual work does not stand apart from the life of faith. It participates in it.

Beyond ethical formation, these guilds also serve a practical function within the life of the diocese. They coordinate expertise for the benefit of Catholic institutions. Lawyers assist in legal structure and

---

[80] Pope Leo XIII, *Rerum Novarum* (Vatican City: Vatican Press, A.D. 1891), §51.
[81] St. Hildegard of Bingen, *Scivias*. Translated by Mother Columba Hart and Jane Bishop (New York: Paulist Press, A.D. 1990), Book I, Vision 3.

arbitration. Engineers contribute to infrastructure and development. Financial professionals guide the stewardship of assets. Educators shape intellectual formation. Physicians support healthcare systems aligned with the dignity of life.

In this way, professional knowledge is no longer confined to external systems. It is reintegrated into the life of the Church. The talents of the faithful become instruments of renewal rather than resources absorbed by institutions indifferent to the moral order.

The Collegiate Guilds therefore represent more than professional associations. They are communities of vocation. They seek to align technical knowledge with moral truth, professional authority with responsibility, and expertise with service to the common good.

They also serve as schools of formation for the next generation. Younger members of each profession are guided by experienced mentors who have already navigated the challenges of their field. In this way, the guild transmits not only knowledge, but judgment. It forms not only competence, but character.

The restoration of such communities would allow Catholic professionals to recover a sense of unity within their lives. Their work would no longer exist in tension with their faith, but in continuity with it. Their expertise would contribute directly to the building of institutions capable of sustaining a Catholic society.

The Labor Guilds

✠ ✠ ✠

No society can endure on professional knowledge alone. Beneath the work of lawyers, physicians, financiers, and educators stands a more fundamental layer of economic life upon which all civilization depends. Food must be grown, buildings constructed, roads maintained, energy produced, and goods transported from place to place. These activities form the material foundation upon which every community rests.

For this reason, the restoration of Catholic civil society must include not only the organization of the learned professions but also the reestablishment of strong vocational communities among those whose labor sustains the physical economy. Farmers, builders, manufacturers, mechanics, drivers, electricians, and countless other skilled workers form the productive backbone of society. Their work feeds cities, constructs homes, and maintains the infrastructure that allows daily life to function.

The dignity of such labor is deeply rooted in the Christian understanding of man's place within creation. From the beginning, man was entrusted with the care of the material world. The Book of Genesis records that the Lord placed man in the garden "to dress it and to keep it."[82] Work was therefore not introduced as a burden imposed upon humanity, but as

[82] The Holy Bible, Translated from the Latin Vulgate, Douay-Rheims Edition (Baltimore: John Murphy Company, A.D. 1899), Genesis 2:15.

part of its original vocation. The cultivation of land, the shaping of materials, and the building of human settlements are expressions of stewardship.

St. John Chrysostom, reflecting on the necessity of labor, observed that "God has made labor necessary for us, not for punishment, but for our good."[83] Work forms the person even as it sustains the community.

For much of Christian history, these occupations were organized through guilds similar to those described earlier in this chapter. Farmers coordinated cultivation and land stewardship within stable communities. Builders and masons formed guilds responsible for constructing homes, bridges, and churches. Craftsmen developed skills through apprenticeship, while merchants and transporters organized the movement of goods between regions.

These structures ensured that production remained rooted in personal responsibility and local knowledge. The farmer knew the land he cultivated. The builder understood the materials he shaped. The craftsman recognized the families who depended upon his work. Economic life remained connected to place, to reputation, and to the moral order that governed the community.

Modern economic systems have gradually weakened these

---

[83] St. John Chrysostom, *Homilies on Genesis*. In *Nicene and Post-Nicene Fathers*, First Series, Volume 11 (New York: Christian Literature Publishing Co., A.D. 1889), Homily 15.

relationships. Large corporate structures now dominate agriculture, manufacturing, transportation, and energy production. Workers often participate in these industries as isolated employees rather than as members of stable vocational communities. The knowledge required to sustain local economies frequently disappears as small farms, independent workshops, and family trades vanish from many regions.

St. John Paul II warned of this condition, noting that "work is for man and not man for work."[84] When economic systems reverse this order, the worker is reduced to a function rather than recognized as a person.

The organization of Labor Guilds offers one means of restoring balance. These guilds gather those engaged in agriculture, construction, manufacturing, logistics, energy production, and land stewardship into communities that cooperate within the life of the diocese.

The Farmers Guild coordinates agricultural production, supports local food networks, and promotes responsible stewardship of land. The Construction Guild brings together builders, masons, electricians, and tradesmen responsible for maintaining and expanding the physical infrastructure of the community. The Manufacturing Guild supports the production of goods necessary for daily life, while the Transportation Guild organizes the movement of resources across the diocesan economy.

---

[84] Pope St. John Paul II, *Laborem Exercens* (Vatican City: Vatican Press, A.D. 1981), §6.

Energy and infrastructure guilds address the systems that sustain modern society, including utilities, power generation, and communications networks. Security and land stewardship guilds protect both physical property and the natural resources upon which long-term stability depends.

The Christian tradition has long insisted that such work must be carried out with both discipline and purpose. St. Joseph, though silent in Scripture, stands as the model of the laboring man, a craftsman whose work sustained the Holy Family and whose fidelity gave dignity to ordinary labor. In him, the life of work is united to obedience, responsibility, and quiet strength.

St. Basil the Great, addressing those who labored with their hands, taught that "the bread which you do not use is the bread of the hungry."[85] Labor, therefore, is not merely productive. It is ordered toward the needs of others.

When work is organized within stable communities guided by moral principles, it strengthens both families and society. Workers gain dignity through mastery of their craft. Communities gain resilience through local production. Economic life becomes more closely aligned with the needs of the people it serves.

The Catechism of the Catholic Church teaches that "human work

[85] St. Basil the Great, *Homily on Avarice*. In *Nicene and Post-Nicene Fathers*, Second Series, Volume 8 (New York: Christian Literature Publishing Co., A.D. 1895), §6.

proceeds directly from persons created in the image of God… work honors the Creator's gifts and the talents received from him."[86] When labor is ordered toward these ends, it becomes a participation in the creative activity of God.

The restoration of Labor Guilds therefore represents an essential element in the rebuilding of Catholic civil society. They reconnect productive work with responsibility, local stewardship, and the life of the Church. Through them, the physical foundations of the diocesan community can once again be strengthened and secured for future generations.

---

[86] Catechism of the Catholic Church (Vatican City: Libreria Editrice Vaticana, A.D. 1992), §2427.

Chapter VII

The Catholic Economy and the Order of Labor

Local Production and Agriculture

✠ ✠ ✠

Every civilization ultimately rests upon the stability of its food supply. However advanced a society may become in technology, finance, or administration, it cannot endure if it loses the capacity to produce the basic necessities of life. Fields must be cultivated, animals raised, food preserved, and harvests distributed. The strength of any economy begins with the land and those who work it.

For much of Christian history, agricultural life formed the stable foundation of society. Villages, towns, and cities developed in continuity with the rhythms of planting and harvest. The Church stood at the center of this life, not only spiritually but materially. Monasteries cultivated land, preserved agricultural knowledge, and sustained surrounding communities. Farmers organized their labor in harmony with the liturgical calendar, and local markets connected producers with those they served. Food was not an abstract commodity. It was the visible fruit of human labor ordered within creation.

Sacred Scripture consistently presents agriculture as a noble vocation. The Book of Proverbs teaches that "he that tilleth his land shall be satisfied with bread."[87] This is not merely an observation about productivity. It is a recognition that honest labor upon the land establishes a direct relationship between the worker, creation, and the sustenance of the community.

St. Isidore of Seville, reflecting on the dignity of agricultural life, wrote that "the cultivation of the earth is the first art of man, and the foundation of all others."[88] Without it, no higher form of society can endure.

In the modern world, this connection between land and community has been significantly weakened. Agricultural production has been consolidated into large-scale systems that operate far removed from the people they serve. Food travels great distances before reaching the

---

[87] The Holy Bible, Translated from the Latin Vulgate, Douay-Rheims Edition (Baltimore: John Murphy Company, A.D. 1899), Proverbs 12:11.
[88] St. Isidore of Seville, *Etymologiae*. Translated by Stephen A. Barney (Cambridge: Cambridge University Press, A.D. 2006), Book XVII.

table, and the knowledge required to cultivate land is increasingly separated from daily life. Farmers often labor under economic pressures shaped by distant markets rather than local needs.

At the same time, many modern practices have introduced forms of instability. Soil is exhausted through overuse, ecosystems are disrupted, and food itself is often reduced to a processed product detached from its natural origin. The pursuit of efficiency, when detached from stewardship, can produce abundance in the short term while undermining sustainability in the long term.

Pope Benedict XVI observed that "the way humanity treats the environment influences the way it treats itself."[89] When the land is treated as a resource alone, the human person is gradually treated in the same way.

The renewal of a Catholic economy must therefore begin with the restoration of local agricultural life. Diocesan communities should support Catholic farmers, encourage responsible stewardship of land, and strengthen local food networks capable of sustaining families in times of both stability and disruption.

One practical step toward this goal is the formation of agricultural cooperatives within the guild structure described in the previous chapter. Farmers, food producers, bakers, and distributors can organize themselves

---

[89] Pope Benedict XVI, *Caritas in Veritate* (Vatican City: Vatican Press, A.D. 2009), §51.

into networks that coordinate production and distribution across the diocese. Such cooperation allows smaller farms to remain viable while preserving local responsibility for food production.

Community cultivation also plays an important role. Parish grounds, unused diocesan land, and shared spaces can be developed into gardens that provide food while forming habits of stewardship. These efforts reconnect families with the rhythms of nature and offer opportunities for education, cooperation, and service.

Food production guilds can extend this work by organizing parish kitchens, small-scale production, and local artisan practices. Bread, preserves, cheeses, and traditional foods can be prepared within communities according to shared standards of quality and integrity. These practices restore not only economic resilience but also cultural memory.

St. Basil the Great, speaking on the use of material goods, reminded his hearers that "the goods of this world are given in common, and it is unjust for one to possess more than he needs while others lack what is necessary."[90] The production and distribution of food must therefore remain ordered toward the needs of the community.

The Church has long taught that economic activity must serve the common good. The Catechism of the Catholic Church teaches that

---

[90] St. Basil the Great, *Homily on Wealth*. In *Nicene and Post-Nicene Fathers*, Second Series, Volume 8 (New York: Christian Literature Publishing Co., A.D. 1895), §8.

"economic life is not meant solely to multiply goods produced and increase profit… it is ordered first of all to the service of persons."[91] A food system rooted in local cooperation reflects this principle more clearly than one governed solely by distant and impersonal forces.

Another element of stability lies in prudent foresight. Throughout history, communities have maintained reserves of food to guard against famine, crop failure, or disruption. In an age of fragile supply chains, such prudence regains its importance. Storage, preservation, and distribution must be considered part of the structure of a resilient economy.

Local production therefore serves both moral and practical ends. It restores responsibility toward the land, strengthens families and communities, and reduces dependence upon systems whose stability cannot always be guaranteed.

The Catholic economy envisioned here does not reject trade or technology. It seeks to order them properly. The essential foundations of life must remain rooted in local stewardship, where human responsibility is visible and accountable.

From the cultivation of the soil arises the stability of society itself. When Catholic communities reclaim stewardship of their land and food production, they begin not simply an economic reform, but a restoration of

---

[91] Catechism of the Catholic Church (Vatican City: Libreria Editrice Vaticana, A.D. 1992), §2426.

order, one that reaches from the earth beneath their feet to the life of the community they sustain.

Infrastructure and Industry

✠ ✠ ✠

If agriculture forms the foundation of economic life, infrastructure and industry provide the structure through which a society grows and sustains itself. Homes must be built, roads maintained, machines repaired, energy produced, and goods manufactured. These activities form the physical framework that allows communities to flourish across generations.

For most of Christian history, these essential tasks were carried out by local craftsmen organized within vocational guilds. Masons constructed churches and homes. Blacksmiths forged tools and hardware. Carpenters, millers, bakers, and wagon builders formed the practical backbone of daily life. These trades were not merely technical occupations but respected vocations that contributed directly to the stability of the community.

Sacred Scripture affirms the dignity and necessity of such labor. The Book of Ecclesiasticus observes that without the work of craftsmen, "the city shall not be inhabited."[92] Civilization itself depends upon those who shape stone, wood, metal, and earth into the structures necessary for human life.

---

[92] The Holy Bible, Translated from the Latin Vulgate, Douay-Rheims Edition (Baltimore: John Murphy Company, A.D. 1899), Ecclesiasticus 38:34.

The Catholic Economy and the Order of Labor

St. Justin Martyr, reflecting on the ordering of human society, noted that material work serves a higher purpose when it contributes to the life of the community. "We who once valued the acquisition of wealth and possessions more than anything else now bring what we have into a common fund and share it with anyone in need."[93] The physical work of production is therefore not isolated from moral responsibility. It is ordered toward the good of others.

Modern industrial systems have expanded the scale and complexity of production beyond anything known in earlier centuries. Factories, global supply chains, and automated technologies produce goods at extraordinary volume. These developments have brought real advantages, yet they have also created economic structures that often separate production from the communities that depend upon it.

Many towns that once supported skilled craftsmen and small manufacturers now rely upon distant corporations for essential goods and services. When such industries relocate or fail, entire regions can lose the economic foundations that sustained them. Workers who once possessed practical trades often become dependent upon employment structures over which they have little control and in which their work is reduced to a narrow function within a much larger system.

---

93 St. Justin Martyr, *First Apology*. In *The Ante-Nicene Fathers*, Volume 1 (Buffalo: Christian Literature Publishing Co., A.D. 1885), Chapter 14.

The Catholic economy envisioned here seeks to restore a healthier balance. It does not reject modern industry, but it insists that the productive capacity of local communities must be strengthened so that they are not entirely dependent upon distant systems. Production must once again be connected to place, to responsibility, and to the people it serves.

Within the diocesan structure, this work belongs primarily to the Labor Guilds. Construction guilds coordinate builders, masons, electricians, plumbers, and tradesmen responsible for maintaining homes, churches, schools, and community facilities. Manufacturing guilds encourage the development of workshops capable of producing essential goods at a scale appropriate to local needs.

Transportation and logistics guilds organize the movement of resources across the diocesan economy. Drivers, mechanics, and planners ensure that food, materials, and goods can move efficiently between communities without reliance upon fragile external systems.

Energy production has become another critical component of modern infrastructure. Electrical systems, fuel networks, and communication technologies form the underlying framework upon which contemporary life depends. Their management requires not only technical expertise but moral responsibility, since entire communities depend upon their stability.

St. John Chrysostom, preaching on the necessity of labor, warned that "nothing is more disgraceful than a Christian who does not work."[94] Infrastructure and industry, therefore, are not merely technical concerns. They are expressions of responsibility. A society that neglects the formation of skilled workers and the cultivation of productive labor undermines its own foundations.

Catholic social teaching has repeatedly warned against the dangers of excessive concentration within economic life. Pope Pius XI taught that "it is an injustice… to assign to a greater and higher association what lesser and subordinate organizations can do."[95] When production is removed from local communities and concentrated in distant systems, both responsibility and participation are weakened. A healthy society therefore strengthens smaller institutions and local forms of economic life rather than relying entirely upon centralized structures.

Practical initiatives within the diocesan economy may take many forms. Parish kitchens and school facilities can serve as centers for small-scale production. Families may gather to prepare traditional foods that reflect the cultural inheritance of the community. Breads, preserves, cheeses, and other goods can be produced according to shared standards that ensure quality, fairness, and integrity.

---

94 St. John Chrysostom, *Homilies on Second Thessalonians*. In *Nicene and Post-Nicene Fathers*, First Series, Volume 13 (New York: Christian Literature Publishing Co., A.D. 1889), Homily 4.
95 Pope Pius XI, *Quadragesimo Anno* (Vatican City: Vatican Press, A.D. 1931), §79.

Such activity strengthens social life as well as economic life. Shared work becomes an occasion for fellowship. Cultural traditions are preserved and transmitted. The economy becomes visible again as a network of relationships rather than an abstract system.

Other forms of production can develop alongside these efforts. Workshops producing devotional items, liturgical furnishings, and sacred art contribute both materially and spiritually to the life of the Church. Craftsmen trained within these guilds preserve traditions that modern industry has largely abandoned.

Construction and maintenance guilds may begin with the care of diocesan property. Parish grounds, schools, and other facilities require continual attention. By organizing local craftsmen to serve these needs, the diocese strengthens both its physical infrastructure and the economic stability of its workers.

From this foundation, such guilds may gradually extend their work into the surrounding community. Those who maintain churches and diocesan buildings may assist in constructing homes, restoring historic structures, and undertaking projects that strengthen the common life of the people.

What begins in service to the Church does not remain confined within it. It becomes the seed of a broader renewal.

The rebuilding of infrastructure and industry within Catholic communities is therefore not merely an economic project. It represents the restoration of a right relationship between work, community, and faith. What is made is once again connected to those for whom it is made, and labor is reoriented toward service rather than abstraction.

As the productive life of the community is strengthened in this way, it becomes possible to turn toward a deeper and more enduring task. The stewardship of the land itself, which underlies every form of economic and social life, must then be considered with care.

Land Stewardship

✠ ✠ ✠

Behind every stable civilization stands a more enduring foundation than markets, institutions, or political systems. That foundation is land. Nations may rise and fall, currencies may fluctuate, and industries may transform with new technologies, but the land upon which a people lives remains the constant ground of their existence. For this reason, the long-term stability of any community depends upon the responsible stewardship of the land entrusted to it.

From the beginning of Sacred Scripture, the care of the earth is presented as part of man's vocation. Creation is not given as an object of domination alone, but as something to be received, cultivated, and preserved. Man stands within creation as both user and guardian, drawing from it what is necessary for life while remaining accountable for its condition.

St. Ambrose expressed this balance with clarity, teaching that "the earth was established in common for all, rich and poor alike."[96] The land therefore carries within it a moral dimension. It is not merely a possession, but a trust.

Christian civilization historically reflected this understanding. Land was cultivated not only for immediate gain, but for continuity. Fields were preserved across generations. Forests were managed with restraint. Water sources were protected. Monasteries and rural parishes often became centers of disciplined stewardship, where agricultural practice was shaped by a deeper vision of order and responsibility.

In the modern industrial age, this sense of stewardship has often been replaced by a more extractive approach. Land is treated as a resource to be consumed rather than a gift to be sustained. Production is measured in short-term yield rather than long-term health. Soil is depleted, waterways are polluted, and landscapes are altered without regard for permanence.

The consequences are no longer abstract. Communities face declining soil fertility, fragile food systems, and environments that no longer support the stability they once provided. The same habits that reduce goods

---

[96] St. Ambrose, *De Nabuthe Jezraelita (On Naboth).* In *Nicene and Post-Nicene Fathers*, Second Series, Volume 10 (New York: Christian Literature Publishing Co., A.D. 1896), Chapter 12.

to disposable objects gradually extend to the land itself, which is used without regard for its future.

St. Hildegard of Bingen, writing with a striking awareness of the harmony within creation, warned that "the earth does not bear what it once did, because man has turned away from its right order."[97] Disorder in human life produces disorder in the natural world.

For Catholic communities seeking to rebuild stable local economies, responsible land stewardship must therefore become a central concern. Dioceses and parishes often possess significant land resources, including church properties, unused fields, former school grounds, and rural parcels held across generations. These lands are not only remnants of the past, but foundations for the future.

A careful survey of diocesan land can reveal opportunities for agricultural development, housing, community use, and restoration. Some properties may support farming cooperatives that strengthen local food production. Others may provide space for orchards, vineyards, or small livestock operations. Still others may be reserved for long-term preservation.

Tree planting and ecological restoration contribute to this work in a direct and visible way. Forests stabilize soil, regulate water, and provide

---

[97] St. Hildegard of Bingen, *Physica*. Translated by Priscilla Throop (Rochester: Healing Arts Press, A.D. 1998), Book I.

continuity across generations. Parish communities can participate in such efforts not only as environmental initiatives, but as acts of stewardship rooted in responsibility.

The cultivation of beauty also belongs within this vision. The Christian tradition has always recognized that beauty is not accidental, but formative. Ordered landscapes, well-kept grounds, and thoughtfully maintained spaces shape the imagination of those who live within them. A place that is cared for teaches care.

St. Bernard of Clairvaux, writing of the natural world, observed that "you will find something greater in the forests than in books; trees and stones will teach you what you cannot learn from masters."[98] Creation itself becomes a teacher when it is preserved and encountered rightly.

Long-term stewardship often requires structures that protect land from fragmentation or misuse. Land trusts and similar arrangements allow communities to preserve farmland, forests, and essential spaces for future generations. Such structures encourage a perspective that extends beyond immediate profit toward lasting stability.

This long view is essential. Land, when properly cared for, continues to provide across centuries. It sustains families, supports communities, and anchors institutions in a way that few other resources

---

[98] St. Bernard of Clairvaux, *Epistolae (Letters)*. In *The Letters of St. Bernard of Clairvaux*. Translated by Bruno Scott James (London: Burns & Oates, A.D. 1953), Letter 106.

can. When neglected, however, it deteriorates in ways that may take generations to repair.

For this reason, stewardship of land must be understood not simply as environmental concern, but as a moral and civilizational responsibility. It reflects a commitment to continuity, to inheritance, and to the well-being of those who will come after.

When the land is treated with care, the community gains stability. When it is neglected, the effects extend far beyond the soil itself.

As agriculture, industry, and land stewardship are brought into proper order, a further question arises. These activities require systems of exchange, credit, and investment capable of sustaining their growth and coordination. The renewal of economic life must therefore also address the structure of finance itself.

Chapter VIII

Finance, Credit, and the Stewardship of Wealth

Catholic Banking Institutions

✠ ✠ ✠

No economic system can function for long without institutions capable of directing credit and capital toward productive activity. Land may exist, workers may possess skill, and communities may desire to build, but without access to financial capital these efforts remain unrealized. The ability to borrow, invest, and coordinate financial resources therefore plays a decisive role in shaping the life of a society.

For much of Christian history, financial activity remained closely tied to the communities it served. Lending occurred within networks of trust. Cooperative funds, guild-based credit, and local banking institutions allowed families and craftsmen to obtain the resources necessary for farms, workshops, and homes. Capital circulated within the same communities from which it arose, reinforcing stability rather than extracting value from it.

In the modern financial system, this relationship has largely disappeared. Savings gathered from local communities are transferred through national and global markets and invested in enterprises far removed from the needs of the people who produced that wealth. Capital becomes abstract. It flows according to scale and return rather than proximity or responsibility.

The result is a paradox that defines much of contemporary economic life. Enormous financial wealth exists in the form of portfolios, funds, and digital assets, yet many families struggle to obtain what earlier generations considered basic. Homes become increasingly inaccessible. Land is consolidated into large holdings. Productive property is treated less as a foundation for life and more as an instrument of speculation.

This condition has direct consequences for family life. When access to property is restricted, stability weakens. Marriage is delayed. Birthrates plumet. Communities lose continuity. Economic life becomes detached from the rhythms of human life.

Pope Leo XIII recognized the importance of widely distributed ownership, writing that "the law… should favor ownership, and its policy should be to induce as many as possible of the people to become owners."[99] Property, when properly distributed, strengthens independence, responsibility, and dignity.

Yet the possession of wealth carries obligations as well as rights. St. Thomas Aquinas teaches that "in regard to external things, man ought not to hold them as his own, but as common, so as to share them without hesitation when others are in need."[100] Wealth is therefore not an end in itself. It is a means ordered toward the common good.

Sacred Scripture speaks with similar clarity. St. James warns against wealth that is hoarded or detached from justice, declaring, "your riches are corrupted… behold the hire of the laborers… which by fraud has been kept back by you, cries out."[101] Financial systems that separate wealth from responsibility ultimately become destructive.

Modern Catholic thinkers also recognized the dangers of financial abstraction. Hilaire Belloc observed that when ownership is removed from the majority of people, society tends toward instability, writing that "the control of the means of production… is the mark of a free society."[102] When capital is concentrated and detached from labor, freedom itself is weakened.

G.K. Chesterton expressed the same insight with characteristic

---

[99] Pope Leo XIII, *Rerum Novarum* (Vatican City: Vatican Press, A.D. 1891), §46.
[100] St. Thomas Aquinas, *Summa Theologiae*. Translated by the Fathers of the English Dominican Province (New York: Benziger Brothers, A.D. 1947), II–II, q. 66, a. 2.
[101] The Holy Bible, Translated from the Latin Vulgate, Douay-Rheims Edition (Baltimore: John Murphy Company, A.D. 1899), James 5:2–4.
[102] Hilaire Belloc, *The Servile State* (London: T. N. Foulis, A.D. 1912), Chapter 2.

clarity: "Too much capitalism does not mean too many capitalists, but too few capitalists."[103] A healthy society is not one in which wealth disappears, but one in which ownership is broadly shared.

The purpose of Catholic banking institutions within the diocesan economy is therefore not to replicate existing financial systems, but to restore the relationship between capital and community. Financial institutions must once again serve the real economy of families, work, and local life.

The most practical instrument for this purpose is the establishment of diocesan credit unions or cooperative financial institutions. Unlike commercial banks, which are accountable primarily to shareholders, credit unions are owned by their members. Depositors participate in the life of the institution, and the benefits of its activity remain within the community.

Within the framework of *Catholic Action*, such institutions could play a central role in rebuilding economic life. Loans can be directed toward Catholic farmers, small businesses, housing initiatives, and infrastructure projects that strengthen local stability.

Mortgage programs can assist young families in obtaining homes within their communities. Agricultural lending can support family farms facing pressure from large industrial competitors. Business loans can enable

---

[103] G.K. Chesterton, *The Outline of Sanity* (London: Methuen & Co., A.D. 1926), Chapter 3.

craftsmen and entrepreneurs to establish enterprises rooted in moral principles rather than purely financial incentives.

Because these institutions operate within a defined community, lending decisions are informed by real knowledge rather than abstract risk models alone. This reduces speculation and encourages responsibility. Borrowers are not anonymous. They are members of the same community.

Keeping capital within the community produces further stability. Savings deposited by families are reinvested locally. Growth strengthens the same people who generated the original wealth. Financial activity becomes visible again as a form of cooperation rather than an impersonal system.

Such institutions also allow for moral clarity in investment. Capital can be directed toward enterprises that respect human dignity and the teaching of the Church, while avoiding industries that undermine it. Finance is thereby reconnected to ethics.

The Church has long warned against financial practices that detach money from real production. The tradition consistently condemned usury not merely as excessive interest, but as the unjust gain derived from money without productive purpose. Money exists to facilitate exchange and support real economic activity. When it becomes an end in itself, it distorts the entire system.

For this reason, the renewal of Catholic economic life requires not only access to capital, but the right ordering of capital. Credit must serve production. Investment must serve community. Wealth must serve the common good.

Financial systems will always exist. The question is whether they will be ordered toward the flourishing of persons or toward the accumulation of power detached from responsibility. By organizing cooperative financial institutions rooted in the life of the diocese, Catholic communities can begin to restore a more just and stable economic order.

The next section will examine another form of financial cooperation that once played a vital role in Christian society: systems of insurance and mutual aid that protected families from hardship while strengthening the bonds of community life.

Catholic Insurance and Mutual Aid

✠ ✠ ✠

Financial stability requires more than access to credit and investment. Every family eventually encounters moments of hardship that cannot be avoided by prudence alone. Illness, injury, death, and economic disruption are enduring features of human life. A healthy society must therefore cultivate institutions capable of protecting families when such burdens arise.

For much of Christian history, this protection did not depend upon large and impersonal systems, but upon networks of mutual aid rooted in local communities. Guilds, confraternities, and parish societies maintained common funds that assisted members in times of need. Widows were not abandoned. Children were not left without support. The vulnerable were sustained by the very communities to which they belonged.

These practices were not accidental. They arose from a distinctly Christian vision of social life. In the Acts of the Apostles, the early Church is described as a community in which "neither was there any one needy among them."[104] The sharing of goods was not merely generosity, but an expression of communion.

St. Gregory the Great expressed this principle with clarity, teaching that "when we give to the poor what is necessary, we are not bestowing alms, but restoring what is theirs."[105] Wealth, therefore, carries an obligation. It is not held absolutely, but in relation to the needs of others within the community.

Over time, these principles took institutional form. Guilds maintained funds to assist members in illness or disability. Confraternities ensured that the dead received proper burial. Parish societies provided for widows and orphans. These were not abstract systems, but communities of care shaped by shared faith and personal knowledge.

---

[104] The Holy Bible, Translated from the Latin Vulgate, Douay-Rheims Edition (Baltimore: John Murphy Company, A.D. 1899), Acts 4:34.
[105] St. Gregory the Great, *Regula Pastoralis (Pastoral Rule)*. Translated by Henry Davis (London: Burns & Oates, A.D. 1950), Book III, Chapter 21.

Such institutions functioned as more than financial arrangements. They embodied fraternity. Members contributed not to an impersonal pool, but to a common life. The one who gave and the one who received often knew one another. Charity was therefore immediate, concrete, and human.

With the rise of industrial society, many of these structures were weakened or replaced. Corporate insurance systems and state welfare programs assumed functions once carried out by local communities. While these systems provided a certain level of material security, they often did so at the cost of social cohesion.

Pope Pius XI identified this problem with precision, warning that when smaller associations are absorbed into larger structures, the organic life of society is diminished. "The social organism," he wrote, "cannot be built up unless it is composed of many smaller and intermediate groups."[106] When these disappear, individuals become increasingly isolated.

For this reason, the renewal of Catholic civil society requires not only economic development, but the restoration of mutual aid. Financial systems must once again be complemented by institutions that bind people together in responsibility and care.

Within the diocesan framework, such systems can take several forms. Life insurance associations may be organized to provide stability for

[106] Pope Pius XI, *Quadragesimo Anno* (Vatican City: Vatican Press, A.D. 1931), §79.

families in the event of death. Disability funds can assist workers who are no longer able to continue in their trade. Burial societies can ensure that families are not burdened in moments of grief.

Healthcare sharing ministries offer another model. By contributing to a common fund governed by shared moral principles, members support one another in times of medical need. These systems avoid many of the ethical conflicts present in conventional insurance, including the funding of procedures contrary to Catholic teaching such as abortion, contraception, sterilization, in vitro fertilization (IVF), and certain forms of end-of-life intervention. They also reduce reliance on bureaucratic approval structures that may pressure patients or physicians to act against conscience. In this way, healthcare becomes not merely a managed service, but a form of mutual care ordered toward both physical well-being and moral integrity.

The deeper value of such institutions lies not only in the assistance they provide, but in the relationships they sustain. When individuals know that their contributions directly support others within their community, generosity becomes integrated into daily economic life. Giving is no longer abstract. It becomes personal.

Christopher Dawson observed that a society is held together not merely by laws or economic arrangements, but by shared beliefs and practices. "Society is not merely a collection of individuals, but a community united by a common life."[107] Mutual aid makes this common life visible.

These systems also restore a proper understanding of security. Modern systems tend to locate security in contracts and institutions alone. Christian society locates it first in relationships. A family is secure not only because it holds a policy, but because it belongs to a community that will not abandon it.

The moral significance of this cannot be overstated. A society that relies entirely upon impersonal systems gradually loses the habits of charity that sustain it. A society that practices mutual aid strengthens both its economic and its moral foundations.

For this reason, the restoration of Catholic insurance and mutual aid is not an optional supplement to economic life. It is an essential component of a society ordered toward the common good. It ensures that prosperity does not isolate, and that hardship does not destroy.

With systems of credit and mutual support established, a final question remains. Capital must not only be preserved and distributed, but directed. Investment determines which industries grow, which communities develop, and which institutions endure.

The next section therefore turns to the question of investment, and

---

[107] Christopher Dawson, *Religion and the Rise of Western Culture* (New York: Sheed & Ward, A.D. 1950), Chapter 1.

to the responsibility of directing wealth toward the long-term flourishing of the Catholic community.

Catholic Investment Networks

✠ ✠ ✠

If credit provides the lifeblood of an economy and mutual aid protects families in times of hardship, investment determines the long-term direction of economic development. The way capital is directed shapes the industries that grow, the communities that flourish, and the institutions that endure across generations. For this reason, the stewardship of investment capital represents one of the most serious responsibilities within economic life.

In the modern financial world, this responsibility has largely been separated from the communities whose wealth is being invested. Retirement funds, pension accounts, and investment portfolios channel vast sums of capital into distant markets governed by criteria of scale, efficiency, and return. The moral and social consequences of these decisions often remain hidden from those whose savings sustain them.

The result is a quiet but significant contradiction. Many individuals who seek to live according to the moral teaching of the Church may unknowingly support industries and practices that contradict it. Capital flows toward enterprises without reference to their effect on human life, the dignity of labor, or the stability of communities.

St. Augustine, reflecting on the ordering of human desire, observed that "those who think riches are their good fall away from the true good."[108] Wealth becomes dangerous when it is pursued without reference to the higher ends that give it meaning. Investment detached from truth becomes disordered, even when it appears successful.

At the same time, modern systems of investment frequently fail to support the very communities from which wealth is drawn. Capital accumulated by families may circulate through global markets while local farms decline, small businesses struggle to secure funding, and younger generations find themselves unable to establish stable households. Wealth becomes mobile, but communities become fragile.

The Catholic tradition has consistently taught that the use of wealth must be governed by moral purpose. St. Bonaventure, reflecting on the proper use of material goods, wrote that "temporal goods are ordered to spiritual goods as means to an end."[109] Wealth is therefore instrumental. It exists to serve a higher order, not to replace it.

This principle finds practical expression in the formation of Catholic investment networks. Within the framework of *Catholic Action*,

---

[108] St. Augustine, *De Civitate Dei (City of God)*. Translated by Marcus Dods (New York: Random House, A.D. 1950), Book XII, Chapter 8.
[109] St. Bonaventure, *Commentary on the Sentences*. In *Opera Omnia*, Volume 2 (Quaracchi: Collegium S. Bonaventurae, A.D. 1885), Book II, dist. 1.

such networks bring together financial professionals, entrepreneurs, and investors who are committed to directing capital in a manner consistent with the moral teaching of the Church.

These networks allow investment to be reconnected with responsibility. Rather than dispersing resources across anonymous markets, capital can be directed toward enterprises that strengthen families, support communities, and respect the dignity of human life.

Such initiatives may include the expansion of Catholic businesses operating within the guild system, the development of agricultural cooperatives, and the financing of housing projects that allow families to remain rooted within their communities. Infrastructure investments may support schools, clinics, and community institutions that contribute to long-term stability.

In this way, investment becomes constructive rather than extractive. It builds rather than displaces.

Catholic investment advisors within these networks play an essential role. Their task is not merely to identify profitable opportunities, but to discern whether those opportunities serve the common good. Financial judgment must therefore be joined to moral judgment.

Christopher Dawson observed that economic life cannot be understood in isolation from the spiritual and cultural order of a society. "A civilization lives by its beliefs and dies when it ceases to believe."[110] Investment decisions, though often treated as technical, ultimately reflect these deeper convictions.

In some cases, cooperative venture funds may be established to support new enterprises emerging from the guild system. Entrepreneurs who possess skill and vision but lack initial capital can receive support from investors committed to the long-term flourishing of the community. Innovation, in this context, is not driven by speculation, but by purpose.

This approach also provides a framework for the development of intentionally Catholic communities. Capital can be directed toward projects that integrate housing, education, parish life, and economic activity within a shared moral vision. Such communities offer a tangible expression of the principles described throughout this work.

Strategic coordination at the diocesan level allows these investments to reinforce one another. Capital is not scattered, but ordered. Each project contributes to a broader structure of economic and social life, strengthening the whole rather than competing within it.

St. Bernardine of Siena, who preached extensively on the moral dimensions of economic life, observed that "the merchant who conducts

---

110 Christopher Dawson, *Religion and the Rise of Western Culture* (New York: Sheed & Ward, A.D. 1950), Chapter 2.

his business justly benefits not only himself but the whole community."[111] Investment, when rightly ordered, shares in this same principle. It extends beyond private gain and contributes to the stability and flourishing of society.

When investment is ordered toward the common good, it becomes a form of stewardship. Capital ceases to be merely a measure of wealth and becomes instead a means of building institutions, supporting families, and sustaining communities across generations.

The renewal of Catholic civil society therefore requires not only the moral formation of individuals, but the wise direction of economic resources. When credit, mutual aid, and investment operate together within a unified framework, economic life begins to reflect the order it is meant to serve.

The next chapter turns from the structure of economic life to another essential dimension of human flourishing: the care of health and the protection of human life within the Catholic community.

---

[111] St. Bernardine of Siena, *Sermons on Economic Life*. In *The Sermons of St. Bernardine of Siena*. Translated by Helen Josephine Robins (Siena: Tipografia S. Bernardino, A.D. 1920), Sermon 15.

Chapter IX

Healthcare and the Care of the Human Person

The Medical Guild

✠ ✠ ✠

Among the many professions that sustain society, few carry responsibilities as weighty as those entrusted to physicians and healthcare professionals. The work of medicine enters directly into the most vulnerable moments of human life. Birth, illness, suffering, and death all pass through the hands of those who care for the sick. For this reason, the organization of medical practice within a coherent moral framework becomes essential for any society that seeks to preserve human dignity.

From the earliest centuries of Christianity, the care of the sick stood at the center of the Church's mission. Hospitals, hospices, and houses of charity emerged not as secondary institutions, but as expressions of the Gospel itself. Bishops organized care for the poor and infirm, and monasteries became places where both body and soul were tended together.

St. Basil the Great, established one of the first organized hospital communities, the Basiliad, where the sick, the poor, and the abandoned were received and cared for. He understood such work not as philanthropy, but as an extension of Christian life. "The care of the sick," he taught, "must be preferred to all other works."[112] In this, the Christian approach to medicine was given a lasting form.

This concern for the sick reflects the example of Christ Himself. The Gospels present healing not as an incidental act, but as a sign of the Kingdom. When the Lord sends His disciples into the world, He commands them not only to teach, but to heal. The restoration of the body becomes a visible expression of the restoration of the whole person.

Within this tradition, physicians were never understood as mere technicians. St. Luke, the physician and evangelist, stands as a witness to the harmony between faith and reason. Medical knowledge and spiritual wisdom are not opposed, but ordered toward a common end.

Over time, this vision gave rise to one of the most extensive systems of care the world has known. Catholic hospitals, religious orders dedicated to nursing, and charitable institutions formed the backbone of healthcare in many regions long before modern systems emerged. Medicine

---

[112] St. Basil the Great, *The Longer Rules*. In *Ascetical Works* (New York: Fathers of the Church, A.D. 1950), q. 55.

was practiced not simply as a profession, but as a vocation rooted in charity.

In the modern world, however, medicine has become increasingly complex and increasingly institutional. Advances in technology have expanded the capacity to treat disease, yet they have also introduced systems in which physicians often exercise limited control over the moral direction of care. Decisions are frequently shaped by administrative structures, insurance frameworks, and regulatory requirements that may not reflect a coherent moral vision.

As a result, healthcare professionals often find themselves navigating profound ethical tensions. Questions surrounding abortion, euthanasia, reproductive technologies such as in vitro fertilization, and the proper care of the dying place physicians at the intersection of competing moral frameworks. In many cases, the pressures of institutional systems can conflict with the obligations of conscience.

St. Gregory of Nazianzus, reflecting on the dignity of the human person, warned against reducing the body to a mere object of manipulation, insisting that "man is a creature ordered toward God, not a thing to be used."[113] When medicine loses sight of this truth, it risks becoming detached from the very person it is meant to serve.

For this reason, the formation of a Medical Guild within the

[113] St. Gregory Nazianzen, *Orations*. In *Nicene and Post-Nicene Fathers*, Second Series, Volume 7 (New York: Christian Literature Publishing Co., A.D. 1894), Oration 14.

diocesan structure becomes essential. Such a guild gathers physicians, nurses, pharmacists, therapists, and healthcare professionals into a community of mutual support and shared ethical commitment.

Within this community, practitioners are no longer isolated. They may consult one another on difficult cases, seek guidance in moments of uncertainty, and strengthen one another in maintaining fidelity to the moral teaching of the Church. The burden of ethical decision-making is carried together.

The Medical Guild also serves a practical function. By coordinating healthcare resources across the diocese, it allows for the development of systems that are both effective and resilient. Physicians and administrators can collaborate in maintaining medical supply reserves, developing emergency response plans, and ensuring continuity of care during times of crisis.

Such coordination proved especially necessary during periods of widespread illness and disruption, when supply chains faltered and the fragility of systems dependent upon distant production became evident. A community capable of organizing its own resources gains not only efficiency, but stability.

Professional standards remain central to this work. Medicine requires not only technical expertise, but moral clarity. The physician must exercise judgment not only about what can be done, but about what ought to be done.

St. John Paul II, reflecting on the vocation of healthcare, emphasized that "the dignity of the human person must be recognized in every stage of life."[114] Medical practice, therefore, must remain ordered toward the protection of life from its beginning to its natural end.

The Medical Guild represents more than a professional association. It forms part of a broader effort to restore the unity of knowledge, practice, and moral purpose. Through it, the care of the sick is reintegrated into the life of the Church, and the work of medicine is once again understood as a participation in the healing mission of Christ.

Through cooperation with other guilds, educational institutions, and charitable organizations, the Medical Guild helps ensure that healthcare remains rooted in a true understanding of the human person. The body is not treated in isolation, but in relation to the soul, the family, and the community.

From this foundation, it becomes possible to extend care more widely. The next section therefore examines how healthcare networks built upon these principles can provide access to medical care that is both affordable and faithful to the moral teaching of the Church.

---

[114] Pope St. John Paul II, *Evangelium Vitae* (Vatican City: Vatican Press, A.D. 1995), §2.

Healthcare Networks

✠ ✠ ✠

While the Medical Guild organizes healthcare professionals, the stability of a community's health depends upon institutions capable of delivering care in ways that are both practical and accessible. Physicians alone cannot sustain a system of care. Clinics, pharmacies, laboratories, and support services must exist to provide treatment that is consistent, affordable, and faithful to the moral principles of the Church.

In the modern world, healthcare has become one of the most complex and costly sectors of economic life. Large hospital systems, pharmaceutical corporations, insurance networks, and regulatory structures shape the provision of care across entire nations. These systems possess significant technological capacity, yet they often operate at a distance from the communities they serve.

For many families, this complexity has produced uncertainty. Costs rise without clarity. Access to physicians becomes limited. Administrative systems obscure the personal dimension of care. At the same time, Catholic patients frequently encounter moral conflicts within institutions that do not recognize the ethical teaching of the Church.

The development of local healthcare networks offers a path toward restoring both accessibility and integrity. By coordinating physicians, clinics, pharmacies, and charitable institutions within the life of the diocese, communities can begin to provide care that is both effective and faithful.

One important model for such networks is the Direct Primary Care clinic. In this structure, patients maintain a direct relationship with their physician through a membership arrangement rather than relying primarily upon complex insurance systems. This allows for continuity of care, greater attention to prevention, and the restoration of the personal relationship between doctor and patient.

Medicine, in this form, begins to recover its proper character. It is no longer mediated primarily through systems, but through persons.

St. John Climacus, writing within the ascetical tradition of the East, observed that "the physician is a servant of God's mercy."[115] The work of healing, therefore, is not merely technical. It participates in a deeper act of care rooted in compassion and responsibility.

Direct Primary Care also reduces the administrative burdens that often hinder the practice of medicine. Physicians are freed to focus more fully on the needs of their patients, while families benefit from clearer costs and more consistent access to care.

Pharmacy cooperatives form another essential component of these networks. By organizing pharmaceutical services within cooperative structures, communities can reduce the cost of essential medications while

---

[115] St. John Climacus, *The Ladder of Divine Ascent*. Translated by Archimandrite Lazarus Moore (London: Faber and Faber, A.D. 1959), Step 26.

maintaining oversight of ethical standards. This ensures that the distribution of medicine remains consistent with the moral teaching of the Church.

Healthcare sharing ministries provide an additional layer of support. Through regular contributions to a common fund, members assist one another in meeting significant medical expenses. These systems preserve a sense of shared responsibility and avoid many of the ethical conflicts present in conventional insurance structures.

Such arrangements reflect the principle of solidarity that has long guided Christian life. St. Paul writes that "if one member suffer any thing, all the members suffer with it."[116] Illness is therefore not borne in isolation. It becomes a concern of the whole community.

Partnerships with hospitals remain necessary for providing specialized and advanced care. Local networks need not attempt to replicate every level of medical service, but they can form relationships with institutions that respect the dignity of the human person. In this way, access to complex care is preserved without compromising moral integrity.

The goal of these networks is not withdrawal from the broader medical system, but the restoration of balance. Local institutions regain the ability to provide primary care, coordinate resources, and guide treatment according to principles that respect both life and conscience.

---

[116] The Holy Bible, Translated from the Latin Vulgate, Douay-Rheims Edition (Baltimore: John Murphy Company, A.D. 1899), 1 Corinthians 12:26.

Healthcare and the Care of the Human Person

St. Camillus de Lellis, who dedicated his life to the care of the sick, urged those who serve in medicine to treat each patient "as if he were Christ Himself."[117] This vision restores the personal dimension of healthcare. The patient is not a case, but a person.

The Church has always recognized care for the sick as a central expression of charity. When communities organize themselves to meet this need, they make visible the unity that binds them together. The structures of care become expressions of love.

The creation of Catholic healthcare networks therefore represents more than an administrative reform. It is a recovery of a humane vision of medicine. By strengthening cooperation among physicians, clinics, pharmacies, and charitable institutions, communities provide care that respects both the physical needs and the moral dignity of the human person.

Yet the work of healing cannot end with the body alone. Illness, suffering, and aging often reveal deeper needs that medicine alone cannot address. The care of the whole person requires attention not only to physical health, but to the spiritual and communal dimensions of human life.

The final section of this chapter therefore turns to the care of the

---

[117] St. Camillus de Lellis, *Writings and Sayings*. In *The Life of St. Camillus de Lellis*. Translated by C. V. King (London: Burns & Oates, A.D. 1913), Chapter 12.

whole person within the life of the Christian community.

Care for the Whole Person

✠ ✠ ✠

Modern medicine has achieved remarkable progress in the treatment of disease. Advances in surgery, pharmaceuticals, diagnostics, and medical technology have allowed physicians to address many conditions that once brought certain death. Yet this success has also revealed a limitation. The health of the human person cannot be reduced to the treatment of the body alone.

Man is not merely a biological organism. He possesses intellect, memory, emotion, conscience, and an immortal soul. When illness enters a life, it touches each of these dimensions. Anxiety, loneliness, grief, and spiritual confusion often accompany physical suffering. A system of care that treats only the body therefore fails to address the full reality of the person.

The Christian tradition has always affirmed the unity of body and soul. Christ did not heal as a technician. He restored the whole person. The Gospel of Mark recounts that He not only cured diseases but also brought peace to those who came to Him in distress. Healing, in the Christian vision, is never merely physical. It is restorative in the deepest sense.

For this reason, the Church has historically approached healthcare as a work that unites medical skill with spiritual care. The earliest Christian hospitals were not only places of treatment but places of prayer. The presence of the chapel at the center of these institutions expressed a profound truth. Healing ultimately comes from God, even when mediated through human hands.

The renewal of Catholic healthcare must recover this integrated vision. Care within the community should include not only treatment for illness, but structures that support mental health, family stability, and spiritual well-being.

Mental suffering has become one of the defining burdens of modern life. Anxiety, depression, addiction, and isolation affect countless individuals. These conditions are often intensified by a fragmented society in which individuals are separated from family, tradition, and stable community life.

Catholic counseling and psychological care must therefore be rooted in a true understanding of the human person. The mind cannot be treated as an isolated mechanism. It is ordered toward truth, goodness, and ultimately toward God.

St. Gregory of Nazianzus expressed this principle with striking clarity when he wrote, "what has not been assumed has not been healed."[118]

---

[118] St. Gregory Nazianzen, *Epistle 101*. In *Nicene and Post-Nicene Fathers*, Second Series, Volume 7 (New York: Christian Literature Publishing Co., A.D. 1894), Epistle 101.

The healing of the human person must therefore extend to every dimension of his being. Any form of care that neglects the soul leaves the work incomplete.

Elder care presents another essential responsibility. As communities age, increasing numbers of men and women require assistance, companionship, and dignity in their later years. Modern society often isolates the elderly, separating them from the life of the family and the community.

The Christian vision offers a different approach. Age is not a burden but a fulfillment. The elderly carry memory, wisdom, and continuity. Their presence anchors a community within its own history.

St. John Paul II observed that "a society that abandons its elderly is a society that has lost its memory."[119] Care for the aged is therefore not merely an act of charity. It is an act of justice.

Programs that support elder care within families, parishes, and local communities strengthen the bonds between generations. They ensure that those who have given their lives in service are not set aside, but honored and cared for with dignity.

Preventive care also forms an essential part of this broader vision. A healthy society does not merely respond to illness. It seeks to prevent it.

---

[119] Pope St. John Paul II, *Letter to the Elderly* (Vatican City: Vatican Press, A.D. 1999), §10.

Education in nutrition, physical activity, and responsible living strengthens families and reduces long-term suffering.

This reflects the classical virtue of prudence. Health is not sustained by reaction alone, but by foresight and discipline.

Yet even the most complete system of physical and psychological care remains insufficient without attention to the spiritual life. Suffering often raises questions that medicine cannot answer. Questions of meaning, of purpose, of mortality.

Here the sacramental life of the Church becomes indispensable.

The Anointing of the Sick, Reconciliation, and the Eucharist provide strength that no medical treatment can supply. They unite suffering with the Cross of Christ and open the horizon of eternal life.

St. Ignatius of Antioch, writing on his way to martyrdom, spoke of the Eucharist as "the medicine of immortality."[120] In this phrase, the Church reveals the deepest dimension of healing. The restoration of the human person is not complete until it is ordered toward eternal life.

The dignity of the human person stands at the center of this vision. Man is created in the image of God, called not only to temporal health but to eternal communion. Care for the human person must therefore respect both the body that suffers and the soul that is destined for glory.

---

[120] St. Ignatius of Antioch, *Letter to the Ephesians*. In *The Apostolic Fathers*. Translated by J. B. Lightfoot and J. R. Harmer (London: Macmillan, A.D. 1891), Chapter 20.

St. Hildegard of Bingen, reflecting on the harmony of creation, wrote that "the human being is the work in which God takes delight."[121] To care for the human person is therefore to participate in that divine regard.

The integration of medical, psychological, and spiritual care represents the fullest expression of Christian healthcare. When communities care for the whole person, they do more than treat disease. They restore meaning, dignity, and hope.

In this way, the healing ministry of Christ continues within the life of the Church, not only through the care of the body, but through the restoration of the whole person. Having considered this vision of healthcare, we now turn to another essential dimension of human flourishing, the formation of families, the practice of charity, and the social bonds that sustain a living community.

---

[121] St. Hildegard of Bingen, *Scivias*. Translated by Mother Columba Hart and Jane Bishop (New York: Paulist Press, A.D. 1990), Book I, Vision 2.

Chapter X

Charity, Family, and the Life of the Community

Charitable Institutions

✠ ✠ ✠

No Christian civilization can endure without charity. Institutions of law, economy, and education may sustain the outward structure of society, but charity preserves its heart. Wherever the Church has flourished, the care of the poor, the sick, the orphaned, and the vulnerable has stood at the center of Christian life.

The obligation to care for those in need appears throughout Sacred Scripture. Christ speaks with unmistakable clarity in the Gospel of Matthew, identifying Himself with the hungry, the stranger, the sick, and the imprisoned. In encountering those who suffer, the Christian encounters not an abstraction, but the living presence of Christ.

This conviction marked the earliest Christian communities. Even their critics observed it. In a world often marked by indifference or cruelty toward the weak, Christians became known for their steadfast care of the poor and abandoned. During times of plague, when many fled the afflicted, Christians remained. Widows were supported, orphans protected, and the sick received care at great personal cost.

From these beginnings emerged institutions that would shape Christian civilization for centuries. Hospitals, orphanages, hospices, and houses of charity grew under the guidance of bishops and religious communities. Charity was not treated as an occasional act, but as a permanent and organized expression of the Gospel.

St. Vincent de Paul, whose life was devoted to the service of the poor, insisted that charity must be marked by reverence as well as generosity. "The poor are our masters," he taught, "and we must love them tenderly and respect them deeply."[122] In this vision, the one who gives is not elevated above the one who receives. Both are drawn into a relationship shaped by humility.

Within the diocesan structure described in this work, charitable institutions continue this tradition. They respond to immediate needs while also seeking to restore stability and dignity to those they serve.

---

[122] St. Vincent de Paul, *Conferences and Writings.* Translated by Joseph Leonard (New York: Newman Press, A.D. 1959), Conference 13.

Charity, Family, and the Life of the Community

Among the most vital of these works are pregnancy centers and maternal support programs. These institutions provide care, counseling, and material assistance to women facing unexpected pregnancies. In doing so, they defend human life at its most vulnerable stage while offering practical support that affirms both mother and child.

Food kitchens and agricultural charity networks address another fundamental need. Through cooperation between farms, parish gardens, and food guilds, communities can provide nourishment to families experiencing hardship. Such efforts often depend upon the quiet generosity of volunteers whose labor ensures that no one is left without daily bread.

Clothing distribution and material aid programs offer further assistance. Parish-based initiatives and charitable centers provide essential goods while preserving the dignity of those who receive them. Charity, when rightly ordered, does not humiliate. It restores.

Yet the Christian tradition has always understood that charity must extend beyond immediate relief. It seeks not only to assist, but to renew.

St. Gregory the Great warned against a form of giving that relieves need without addressing its causes, observing that "he who gives to the poor should strive to ensure that poverty itself is relieved."[123] True charity looks beyond the moment. It seeks the restoration of the person.

---

[123] St. Gregory the Great, *Homilies on the Gospels*. In *Nicene and Post-Nicene Fathers*, Second Series, Volume 12 (New York: Christian Literature Publishing Co., A.D. 1895), Homily 20.

For this reason, charitable work must be connected to opportunities for growth and participation. Programs that unite assistance with meaningful work often restore a sense of purpose that mere provision cannot supply. Individuals who receive support may contribute through service within parish life, agricultural work, or community projects. In this way, dignity is not only preserved but strengthened.

Rehabilitation and addiction recovery programs form another essential dimension of this work. Addiction fractures both the individual and the family, often isolating those who suffer from the very relationships that might sustain them. Recovery requires more than treatment. It requires community, discipline, and hope.

St. John of the Cross, reflecting on the transformation of the human person, wrote that "the soul must be healed in order to love rightly."[124] This healing is not immediate. It unfolds over time through guidance, perseverance, and grace.

The Church's teaching consistently affirms that charity must uphold both the dignity and the responsibility of the human person. Love for the poor is not optional. It belongs to the very structure of Christian life. At the same time, charity must be ordered toward restoration, enabling individuals to reenter the life of the community with renewed strength.

---

[124] St. John of the Cross, *Dark Night of the Soul*. Translated by E. Allison Peers (London: Burns & Oates, A.D. 1959), Book I, Chapter 1.

When practiced in this way, charity transforms both the one who gives and the one who receives. It binds individuals together, strengthens communities, and reflects the love that stands at the center of the Gospel.

Yet even the most well-ordered charitable institutions cannot fully address the deeper challenge of social fragmentation. Many who suffer are not only in need of material assistance, but are also separated from stable patterns of work, education, and communal life. The next section turns to this question, examining how Catholic communities can help individuals recover their place within the common life through participation, formation, and meaningful labor.

Community Integration and Social Stability

✠ ✠ ✠

Charity relieves immediate suffering, but a healthy society must also provide paths through which individuals return to stable participation in the common life. Poverty, displacement, addiction, unemployment, and cultural dislocation often separate individuals not only from material security, but from the structures that give life meaning and direction. The work of charity must be joined to institutions capable of restoring persons to roles marked by dignity, responsibility, and belonging.

This task reflects the pattern of Christ's own ministry. The Lord did not merely heal the sick or forgive sins in isolation. He restored persons to communion. The outcast was brought back into the community. The sinner was returned to the life of the people. Healing, in this sense, was not complete until the person was reintegrated into a living relationship with others.

At the heart of this vision lies a fundamental truth about the human person. Man is not made for isolation. He is ordered toward participation in family, work, and community. When these bonds are broken, suffering deepens. The loss is not only economic, but existential.

St. John Paul II described work as one of the primary ways in which the human person expresses his dignity, writing that "through work man not only transforms nature, but achieves fulfillment as a human being."[125] To be separated from meaningful labor is to be separated, in part, from one's own vocation.

For this reason, reintegration into the life of work stands at the center of social restoration. The guild system provides a natural structure for this task. Through apprenticeship and mentorship, individuals who have experienced disruption can gradually regain both skill and confidence. Work performed within a community restores more than income. It restores identity.

Those who have endured unemployment, addiction, or

---

[125] Pope St. John Paul II, *Laborem Exercens* (Vatican City: Vatican Press, A.D. 1981), §9.

incarceration often require more than opportunity. They require accompaniment. St. Benedict, in his Rule, urged that those who have fallen be restored with great care, writing that the superior must "use every possible means to heal the sick soul… and show the greatest concern, lest he lose one of the sheep entrusted to him."[126] Restoration is not achieved through severity alone, but through patient guidance joined to firm direction. Communities that unite discipline with mercy are far more capable of fostering lasting change.

The reintegration of immigrants and newcomers presents another essential dimension of this work. Throughout American history, Catholic parishes served as the primary point of entry into both spiritual and social life. They provided not only worship, but language, education, and connection.

This tradition remains vital. Programs rooted in parish life can assist newcomers in learning the language, understanding civic structures, and forming relationships within the community. At the same time, such efforts allow cultural traditions to be preserved and integrated rather than erased.

St. Augustine described a true society as "a multitude united by a

[126] St. Benedict of Nursia, *The Rule of St. Benedict*. Translated by Rev. Boniface Verheyen (London: Burns & Oates, A.D. 1875), Chapter 27.

common agreement on the objects of their love."[127] Integration, in this sense, is not merely economic or legal. It is the gradual sharing in a common life, a common culture, and a common orientation toward what is good. When newcomers are welcomed into this shared life, the community itself is strengthened. Integration is not a concession. It is an enrichment.

Stable housing forms another necessary foundation. Without it, all other efforts remain fragile. Transitional housing programs can provide the security needed for individuals to rebuild their lives. Yet these programs must be ordered toward reintegration, not isolation. The goal is always a return to permanent participation in the life of the community.

As individuals regain stability, they often become sources of renewal for others. Those who have passed through hardship frequently possess a capacity for compassion and perseverance that strengthens the entire community. Their presence becomes a living testimony that restoration is possible.

St. Leo the Great reflected on the unity of the Christian community by teaching that "the dignity of each member is bound up with the good of the whole."[128] No one is restored in isolation. The healing of one contributes to the strengthening of all.

---

[127] St. Augustine, *De Civitate Dei (City of God)*. Translated by Marcus Dods (New York: Random House, A.D. 1950), Book XIX, Chapter 24.

[128] St. Leo the Great, *Sermons*. In *Nicene and Post-Nicene Fathers*, Second Series, Volume 12 (New York: Christian Literature Publishing Co., A.D. 1895), Sermon 63.

The Church's social teaching consistently affirms that society must be ordered in such a way that individuals are able to participate fully in its life. This participation is not merely economic. It includes relationships, responsibilities, and a sense of belonging.

When reintegration is approached in this manner, it becomes more than a social program. It becomes an act of restoration. Persons are not simply assisted. They are returned to themselves.

From this foundation, a deeper task emerges. A society may succeed in restoring individuals to stability, yet still lack the cultural life that allows families and friendships to flourish. The question is no longer only how people survive, but how they live together.

The final section of this chapter turns to this question, examining the formation of a Catholic social culture in which daily life itself becomes an expression of communion.

Family Life, Fraternity, and Catholic Social Culture

✠ ✠ ✠

The strength of any civilization rests upon the stability of its families and the vitality of its common life. Laws, economic systems, and charitable institutions may sustain the outward framework of society, but it is within the daily life of families and friendships that culture is truly formed. When these foundations weaken, the deeper inheritance of a people begins to fade.

The renewal of Catholic civil society must extend into this ordinary yet decisive sphere. It is here, in the rhythms of daily life, that persons learn how to love, how to live together, and how to hand on what they have received.

Family life stands at the center of this order. The Church has always taught that the family is the first school of virtue and the first place where the faith is lived. Within the home, children encounter authority, sacrifice, forgiveness, and love in their most immediate forms. What is learned here shapes the whole of life.

St. John Chrysostom urged parents to recognize the gravity of this responsibility, calling the home "a little Church."[129] In this image, the family is not merely a private arrangement. It is a living cell of the larger body, a place where the life of the Church takes root.

The formation of families begins long before marriage. Young men and women require communities in which they can encounter one another, form friendships, and grow within a shared moral vision. Modern culture often isolates this stage of life, placing it within environments shaped by distraction and instability.

Catholic communities must recover spaces where relationships can

---

[129] St. John Chrysostom, *Homily on Ephesians*. In *Nicene and Post-Nicene Fathers*, First Series, Volume 13 (New York: Christian Literature Publishing Co., A.D. 1889), Homily 20.

develop within a context of meaning. Parish gatherings, shared work within guilds, cultural events, and acts of service provide natural settings in which friendships mature and vocations emerge. Marriage, in such a setting, arises not from chance, but from participation in a common life.

Human beings are made for communion. The Book of Genesis speaks with simplicity and depth when it declares that it is not good for man to be alone. This truth extends beyond the individual. A society that fails to cultivate relationships becomes fragile, no matter how advanced its institutions.

Fraternal associations strengthen this communal life. Throughout Christian history, confraternities and sodalities allowed individuals to unite around prayer, service, and mutual support. These groups formed bonds that extended beyond the family while remaining rooted in the life of the Church.

Such associations remain essential. Men's groups, women's societies, and guild-based fraternities provide opportunities for mentorship, accountability, and friendship. They cultivate a shared identity that strengthens both the individual and the community.

Celebration also belongs to this life. The liturgical year has always shaped not only worship, but culture. Feasts, processions, shared meals, and public celebrations express the joy of the faith in visible form. They remind communities that the Christian life is not only a path of discipline, but also of delight.

Josef Pieper, a twentieth-century Catholic philosopher who wrote extensively on the relationship between leisure and culture, observed that "leisure is the basis of culture."[130] A society that loses the ability to celebrate loses the ability to remember what it is. Festivals and communal gatherings restore this dimension of life, allowing faith to be experienced not only in doctrine, but in joy.

These celebrations carry memory. Traditions brought by earlier generations remain alive in music, food, language, and devotion. They bind past and present together, giving continuity to the life of the community.

Public acts of devotion further strengthen this identity. Processions, pilgrimages, and Eucharistic adoration make the faith visible within the wider world. They proclaim that religion is not confined to private belief, but belongs to the life of the community.

The formation of youth remains central to this culture. Young people require environments in which they can grow in discipline, friendship, and purpose. Sports, educational programs, and parish activities provide opportunities for formation that extend beyond the classroom.

The cultivation of the sacred arts gives this culture its highest expression. Architecture, music, literature, and visual art reveal the harmony

---

130 Josef Pieper, *Leisure: The Basis of Culture*. Translated by Alexander Dru (New York: Pantheon Books, A.D. 1952), Chapter 1.

between truth, goodness, and beauty. They elevate the imagination and direct it toward God.

Pope Benedict XVI wrote that "the encounter with beauty can become the wound of the arrow that strikes the heart and awakens it to seek what is above."[131] Beauty draws the soul beyond itself. It invites contemplation and restores a sense of order.

Efforts to restore sacred music, support artistic formation, and encourage cultural expression rooted in the faith help ensure that the life of the community remains connected to its deepest sources. Through these works, the invisible truths of the faith become visible.

The purpose of all these activities is not mere diversion. It is the cultivation of a living culture. When families gather, friendships deepen, traditions are celebrated, and beauty is created, the faith becomes woven into the ordinary fabric of life.

St. Aelred of Rievaulx, reflecting on spiritual friendship, wrote that "here we are, you and I, and I hope that Christ makes a third."[132] Friendship, in this sense, becomes a participation in charity itself. It binds individuals together in a unity that reflects the life of the Church.

The renewal of Catholic civilization depends upon this renewal of

---

[131] Pope Benedict XVI, *Meeting with Artists, Sistine Chapel* (Vatican City: Vatican Press, A.D. 2009).
[132] St. Aelred of Rievaulx, *Spiritual Friendship*. Translated by Mary Eugenia Laker (Kalamazoo: Cistercian Publications, A.D. 1977), Book I, Chapter 20.

social life. Families, friendships, festivals, and shared practices form the living heart of the community. Without them, institutions become hollow. With them, society becomes resilient.

With the structures of charity, reintegration, and social life now established, the next chapter turns to another essential responsibility of a stable society, the maintenance of justice, security, and order within the life of the community.

Chapter XI

Law, Security, and the Defense of Christian Society

Legal Systems and Arbitration

✠ ✠ ✠

No society can endure without justice. Communities may possess strong families, productive economies, and charitable institutions, yet if conflicts cannot be resolved fairly, the bonds of trust that sustain social life gradually weaken. Disputes over contracts, property, employment, and responsibility inevitably arise wherever human beings cooperate. For this reason, every stable civilization must develop institutions capable of administering justice and resolving conflicts in an orderly and principled manner.

From the earliest centuries of Christianity, the Church encouraged believers to resolve disputes within their own communities whenever possible. St. Paul addressed this issue directly when writing to the Christians of Corinth. He expressed astonishment that members of the Church would bring their disagreements before pagan courts rather than seeking judgment from fellow believers. "Dare any of you, having a matter against another, go to be judged before the unjust, and not before the saints?"[133] His concern was not merely procedural but moral. Justice, when rooted in a shared understanding of truth and charity, becomes not only a verdict but a means of restoring communion.

Throughout Christian history this principle gave rise to various forms of ecclesiastical and communal arbitration. Guilds, parishes, and confraternities maintained internal mechanisms for resolving disputes among their members. Councils of respected men, often seasoned by experience and formed by the moral teaching of the Church, would hear grievances and render judgments. These were not merely technical decisions, but acts of prudence ordered toward peace.

Such systems served several purposes. They resolved disputes quickly, reduced the burden of prolonged litigation, and preserved the relationships necessary for continued cooperation. Because participants shared a common moral framework, the aim extended beyond determining fault. It sought reconciliation, restitution, and the restoration of right order

---

[133] The Holy Bible, Translated from the Latin Vulgate, Douay-Rheims Edition (Baltimore: John Murphy Company, A.D. 1899), 1 Corinthians 6:1.

between persons.

Within the structure of *Catholic Action*, a similar system of arbitration provides an essential foundation for the economic and social life of the diocese. The Legal Guild gathers lawyers, judges, and legal scholars capable of guiding the community in matters of law and justice. Their task is not only technical but moral, ensuring that legal structures reflect the dignity of the human person and the demands of the common good.

One of the primary responsibilities of this guild is the development of clear and standardized contracts for businesses, guild members, and charitable institutions. Sound agreements prevent conflict before it arises by establishing expectations regarding responsibility, compensation, ownership, and obligation. Clarity in agreement becomes the first safeguard of justice.

When disputes do occur, an internal arbitration board composed of qualified professionals can review the matter and assist the parties in reaching a just resolution. Such boards do not replace civil authority, but they provide a first recourse grounded in shared moral principles. They allow disputes to be addressed with both competence and charity, preserving unity wherever possible.

At the heart of this system lies the classical understanding of justice itself. St. Augustine defined justice as "that virtue which gives to each his due."[134] Without this virtue, no structure of law can sustain peace. Legal systems may multiply rules and procedures, yet if they are detached from moral truth, they become instruments of power rather than guardians of order.

Arbitration rooted in justice also alleviates the heavy burdens often associated with modern legal systems. Civil courts, though necessary, can be slow, costly, and adversarial. When disputes are addressed within a community that values both truth and charity, solutions are often reached more swiftly and with less division.

Legal professionals within the Catholic network also provide guidance to institutions seeking to operate faithfully within both civil law and the moral teaching of the Church. Questions of governance, liability, compliance, and organizational structure require careful attention. Expertise in these matters allows Catholic institutions to act with confidence and integrity in a complex legal environment.

In the modern world, legal systems are not always neutral instruments of justice. Increasingly, they are used as tools of pressure against institutions that operate according to moral principles at odds with prevailing cultural norms. Regulatory burdens, selective enforcement, litigation, and administrative actions can be employed not only to correct

---

[134] St. Augustine, *De Civitate Dei (City of God)*. Translated by Marcus Dods (New York: Random House, A.D. 1950), Book XIX, Chapter 21.

wrongdoing but to gradually weaken or dismantle organizations that refuse to conform. This form of legal pressure, often subtle and indirect, requires a response grounded in both prudence and foresight. A well-formed Legal Guild provides precisely this protection. By maintaining a body of competent legal professionals within the life of the diocese, the community gains the ability to anticipate legal challenges, defend its institutions, and structure its activities in ways that remain faithful to both civil law and moral truth. In this way, legal expertise becomes not merely reactive but protective, safeguarding the long-term stability of Catholic institutions against pressures that might otherwise erode them over time.

The Catechism teaches that "authority is exercised legitimately only when it seeks the common good of the group concerned and if it employs morally licit means to attain it."[135] This responsibility does not belong solely to the state. It is shared, in proper measure, by smaller communities and associations that participate in the ordering of social life. When justice is cultivated at the local level, the entire society is strengthened.

By organizing legal expertise within the life of the diocese, Catholic communities gain the ability to conduct their affairs with clarity and trust. Agreements are honored, disputes are resolved fairly, and cooperation becomes more stable because participants know that justice is present and

---

[135] Catechism of the Catholic Church (Vatican City: Libreria Editrice Vaticana, A.D. 1992), §1903.

active among them.

In this way the administration of justice is no longer experienced as something distant or impersonal. It becomes part of the moral life of the community itself, an expression of the order that reflects the wisdom of God.

Yet law alone cannot preserve social order. Justice must be accompanied by the prudent defense of persons and institutions. Communities must be prepared to safeguard their families, their property, and their common life from threats both visible and unseen. The next section turns to the question of security and the responsible protection of Christian society.

Security and Protection

✠ ✠ ✠

Justice provides the moral foundation of society, but order must also be protected in practical ways. Communities that build institutions, churches, schools, and charitable works must also ensure that these institutions remain safe and secure. Without reasonable protection, the labor and sacrifice of generations can be weakened or destroyed by neglect, disorder, or hostility.

Throughout history Christian communities have recognized the necessity of safeguarding the places that sustain their common life.

Churches, monasteries, and charitable houses stood not only as centers of prayer but as centers of learning, charity, and social organization. To protect them was not merely an act of preservation, but a duty owed to both the faithful and to those yet to come.

Sacred Scripture itself affirms the importance of vigilance. In the Gospel of Luke, Christ observes that if the master of the house knew the hour when the thief would come, he would remain watchful and not allow his house to be broken into.[136] Prudence requires not only good intentions, but foresight. What is entrusted must be guarded.

In the modern world, the forms of risk facing communities have multiplied. Churches and religious institutions have increasingly experienced vandalism, theft, and at times even targeted violence. Alongside these visible threats, new vulnerabilities have emerged within digital systems. Financial records, communications, and personal data are now stored and transmitted through networks that require constant protection.

For this reason, Catholic communities must take seriously the responsibility of safeguarding the institutions they have built. Security is not an expression of hostility, but of stewardship. Buildings raised through the sacrifice of earlier generations deserve careful protection so that they may continue to serve the faithful across time.

---

[136] The Holy Bible, Translated from the Latin Vulgate, Douay-Rheims Edition (Baltimore: John Murphy Company, A.D. 1899), Luke 12:39.

Within the framework of *Catholic Action*, this responsibility can be organized through a coordinated network of trained volunteers and professionals. Members of a Security Guild, together with law enforcement personnel, cybersecurity specialists, and emergency responders, can cooperate to ensure that churches, schools, and community facilities remain protected.

Physical security remains one of the most visible aspects of this work. Parish safety teams can assist in monitoring church grounds during large gatherings, maintaining awareness of potential risks, and ensuring that access to facilities remains orderly and safe. When carried out with discretion and professionalism, such measures support rather than disrupt the life of the community.

Emergency preparedness also forms an essential component of responsible protection. Natural disasters, severe weather, and unexpected crises can disrupt ordinary life with little warning. Communities that establish clear communication systems, emergency plans, and supply reserves are better equipped to respond with calm and coordination when such events arise.

Cybersecurity has become equally necessary. Parishes, schools, financial institutions, and charitable organizations rely upon digital systems for daily operations. Protecting these systems from fraud, intrusion, and data loss requires specialized knowledge. Professionals within the guild structure can provide the expertise necessary to safeguard these networks and ensure their integrity.

At the heart of these efforts lies the virtue of prudence. Hilaire Belloc warned that "the Faith is Europe, and Europe is the Faith,"[137] reminding his readers that a civilization cannot be separated from the principles that sustain it. When those principles are neglected or left undefended, the structures built upon them begin to weaken. Security, rightly understood, is not merely the protection of property, but the preservation of a way of life. It does not arise from fear, but from a clear recognition of responsibility for what has been entrusted to the community.

Cooperation with lawful civil authorities remains essential. Police, emergency services, and public safety officials provide resources and expertise that assist in maintaining order and responding to crises. Catholic communities strengthen their own efforts when they work in harmony with these institutions, respecting their proper authority while contributing to the common good.

The Catechism teaches that public authority exists to ensure the security of society and the conditions necessary for human flourishing.[138] This responsibility is shared, in appropriate measure, by smaller

---

137 Hilaire Belloc, *Europe and the Faith* (London: Constable & Company, A.D. 1920), Chapter 1.
138 Catechism of the Catholic Church (Vatican City: Libreria Editrice Vaticana, A.D. 1992), §2237.

communities and associations. When exercised with prudence and charity, these efforts contribute to a more stable and ordered society.

Security must always remain proportionate and guided by charity. The goal is not to create suspicion, but to preserve peace. Families should be able to worship, learn, and gather without fear. When protection is exercised wisely, it remains largely unseen, allowing the ordinary life of the community to unfold without disruption.

In this way, the safeguarding of institutions becomes an act of fidelity. It ensures that the work of the present generation is not lost, and that the foundations of Christian life remain intact for those who follow.

Yet justice and security alone cannot sustain the moral life of an economic community. Trust must also exist between producers and consumers, employers and workers, businesses and families. The final section of this chapter turns to the role of ethical standards and certification in preserving that trust within the Catholic economy.

The Benedictus Seal

✠ ✠ ✠

The Benedictus Seal proposed in this book draws upon this historical tradition while adapting it to the modern Catholic economy. The word *Benedictus* comes from Latin and means "blessed" or "spoken well of." In Sacred Scripture this language of blessing is frequently directed toward

God Himself: "Blessed be the Lord my God."[139] The term signifies something set apart for good and ordered toward the service of God. Applied to economic life, the Benedictus Seal represents an enterprise whose practices seek to reflect that same moral orientation.

In earlier centuries the guild mark served a similar purpose. Craftsmen stamped their work with the symbol of their guild as a sign that the product had been made according to recognized standards of quality and honesty. The mark represented not merely the reputation of the individual craftsman but the honor of the guild itself. A dishonest merchant or careless craftsman would bring disrepute upon the entire community of his profession. For this reason, guilds carefully guarded their symbols and enforced the standards associated with them.

The Benedictus Seal serves a comparable function within the Catholic economy. It indicates that a business has committed itself to operating according to ethical principles consistent with the moral teaching of the Church. Workers receive just wages and fair treatment. Goods are produced through honest labor rather than exploitation. Supply chains avoid practices that violate human dignity, including forced labor and unjust working conditions. Financial practices remain transparent and ordered toward responsibility rather than speculation detached from the common

---

[139] The Holy Bible, Translated from the Latin Vulgate, Douay-Rheims Edition (Baltimore: John Murphy Company, A.D. 1899), Psalm 143:1.

good.

Such systems of ethical certification are not unfamiliar in the modern world. Other religious communities have long maintained standards that guide the economic life of their members. Jewish communities observe kosher regulations governing the preparation and handling of food according to religious law, while Muslim communities maintain halal certification to ensure that products conform to Islamic moral and ritual requirements. These systems allow believers to participate in modern economic life without abandoning the ethical principles of their faith. The Benedictus Seal offers Catholics a similar means of recognizing businesses that seek to operate within the moral framework of the Church.

In the modern economy, such clarity has become increasingly necessary. Many Catholics unknowingly support industries and corporations whose practices directly contradict the moral teaching of the Church. Investment funds may finance companies that profit from abortion, pornography, or exploitative labor. Supply chains may depend upon factories operating under unjust conditions. Even ordinary consumer goods may originate from economic systems that treat human beings merely as instruments of production. Because modern markets are vast and complex, individuals rarely know how their purchasing decisions influence these broader structures. A certification such as the Benedictus Seal restores a measure of moral clarity by allowing consumers to recognize businesses that have intentionally committed themselves to operating according to Catholic ethical standards.

Sacred Scripture speaks directly to the moral obligations of economic life. "A deceitful balance is an abomination before the Lord: and a just weight is his will."[140] Justice in exchange is not merely a technical matter but a moral one, rooted in truth and honesty before God. Economic activity becomes disordered when profit is pursued through practices such as deceitful marketing, the concealment of defects, manipulation of prices or information, exploitation of asymmetrical knowledge, or the imposition of excessive margins that take advantage of necessity rather than reflect the true value of goods and labor. In such cases, what appears to be success in the marketplace represents a failure of justice.

This principle has been consistently reaffirmed within the Church's social teaching. As Pope Benedict XVI observed, "The economy needs ethics in order to function correctly—not any ethics whatsoever, but an ethics which is people-centred."[141] Economic life cannot be sustained by efficiency alone. It requires trust, and trust depends upon moral integrity.

The Benedictus Seal therefore functions not merely as a commercial label but as a visible sign within the marketplace. It calls both producers and consumers to a higher standard. It encourages Catholics to

---

140 The Holy Bible, Translated from the Latin Vulgate, Douay-Rheims Edition (Baltimore: John Murphy Company, A.D. 1899), Proverbs 11:1.
141 Pope Benedict XVI, *Caritas in Veritate* (Vatican City: Vatican Press, A.D. 2009), §45.

support enterprises that respect human dignity while helping businesses committed to ethical practices earn the trust of the community. Over time such standards can strengthen the entire Catholic economic network, forming habits of honesty, responsibility, and mutual accountability.

In this way, economic life itself becomes more fully integrated into the moral and spiritual order. What is produced, exchanged, and consumed is no longer separated from what is believed. The marketplace, rightly ordered, becomes not only a place of transaction, but a place where the principles of justice and charity are made visible in daily life.

Chapter XII

The Renewal of Catholic Civilization

Financial Sovereignty

✠ ✠ ✠

Economic stability has always formed one of the enduring foundations of civilization. Communities that cannot govern their financial life gradually become dependent upon outside institutions whose priorities may not reflect their own moral or cultural commitments. In time, such dependence weakens not only economic strength, but also the freedom necessary to preserve a distinct way of life. For this reason, the renewal of Catholic civil society requires the recovery of a measured degree of financial sovereignty within the diocesan network.

Throughout Christian history the Church often served as a stabilizing force within economic life. Monasteries preserved agricultural production during periods of social collapse. Cathedral chapters maintained charitable funds for widows, the poor, and the sick. Guilds established systems of mutual credit and shared risk that allowed craftsmen and merchants to operate within a framework of trust and moral accountability. Economic life remained closely connected to the moral authority of the community rather than being detached from it.

Modern financial systems have grown increasingly centralized and abstract. Wealth now frequently exists not in tangible productive assets, but in complex instruments, speculative markets, and distant investment structures. Families often possess little direct influence over the institutions that govern their economic security. Savings are placed into retirement accounts tied to markets that remain opaque, while local businesses depend upon credit systems controlled by entities far removed from the communities they affect.

For this reason, the diocesan economy described in earlier chapters must develop financial institutions capable of supporting its internal activity. A diocesan credit union forms a natural beginning. Organized on cooperative principles, such institutions allow members to pool resources for lending, savings, and financial services. In doing so, financial life begins to return to local stewardship rather than remaining entirely dependent upon distant corporate structures.

Over time this foundation may develop into a broader financial network capable of sustaining the internal life of the community. Digital systems can facilitate efficient transactions between businesses, guild members, and charitable organizations while maintaining transparency and accountability. These tools also allow for the coordination of charitable giving, the regularization of tithing, and the circulation of capital within the Catholic economy rather than its immediate dispersal into external systems.

Advances in financial technology have made possible systems that would have been difficult to imagine in earlier generations. Secure digital ledgers allow for accurate and transparent record-keeping while reducing administrative complexity. Within a properly governed diocesan structure, such technologies could support internal systems of credit used among Catholic institutions and enterprises.

A more developed stage of this system would include the gradual reduction of total dependence on national currencies whose value is determined by distant authorities. Modern fiat currencies remain necessary for participation in the broader economy, yet their inherent instability, particularly through inflationary expansion, limits their reliability as long-term stores of value. A mature Catholic economic network may therefore seek to conduct a portion of its internal transactions through instruments rooted more directly in the life of the community.

Models for such systems already exist. Corporations, digital platforms, and financial networks regularly operate internal credit systems that circulate within their own structures. In a similar manner, a diocesan network could develop internal credits or asset-backed instruments supported by real economic activity within the community.

Unlike speculative systems detached from productive life, such instruments would be grounded in tangible realities: financial reserves, productive enterprises, and land held in stewardship. Their stability would arise not from market speculation, but from their connection to the real goods and services produced by the community itself. In this way, finance remains anchored to reality rather than drifting into abstraction.

Sacred Scripture consistently warns against forms of wealth detached from labor and responsibility. "Wealth gotten hastily shall be diminished: but that which by little and little is gathered with labor shall increase."[142] Stability arises through patience, discipline, and the steady accumulation of value rooted in real work.

The Church has likewise emphasized that financial systems must remain ordered toward the common good. The Catechism teaches that economic activity must respect the dignity of the human person and be directed toward the good of society as a whole.[143] Profit retains its legitimacy, but it cannot stand as the sole measure of economic life when it is separated from justice and responsibility.

Hilaire Belloc observed with characteristic clarity that "control over

---

[142] The Holy Bible, Translated from the Latin Vulgate, Douay-Rheims Edition (Baltimore: John Murphy Company, A.D. 1899), Proverbs 13:11.
[143] Catechism of the Catholic Church (Vatican City: Libreria Editrice Vaticana, A.D. 1992), §2426.

the production of wealth is control over human life itself."[144] When financial systems become detached from the communities they serve, this control shifts away from families and local institutions toward distant and often impersonal powers. The restoration of financial sovereignty is therefore not merely an economic question, but a matter of human freedom and social stability.

When financial life is ordered according to these principles, it ceases to function merely as a mechanism of accumulation. It becomes instead an instrument that supports families, strengthens institutions, and sustains the long-term life of the community. Within such a framework, economic activity once again serves the person rather than subordinating the person to the system.

The renewal of Catholic civilization requires not only spiritual vitality but also economic structures capable of sustaining that vitality across generations. Financial sovereignty within the diocesan network does not imply isolation from the broader economy. It represents a restoration of balance, ensuring that the material foundations of Catholic life remain stable, accountable, and ordered toward the common good.

From this foundation, attention turns naturally to another enduring source of stability: the stewardship and protection of land across

---

[144] Hilaire Belloc, *An Essay on the Restoration of Property* (London: Sheed & Ward, A.D. 1936), Chapter 1.

generations.

The Land Trust and Long-Term Stability

✠ ✠ ✠

If financial sovereignty provides stability for economic exchange, land provides stability for civilization itself. Money moves through markets with speed and abstraction, but land anchors a people to place, memory, and future. A society that loses its connection to land gradually loses its continuity. For this reason, the long-term stability of Catholic civilization cannot rest upon financial institutions alone. It must also rest upon the wise and deliberate stewardship of land.

Throughout history the Church has recognized the importance of land as a foundation of social life. Monasteries cultivated fields, preserved forests, and transformed entire regions through patient labor. Parish lands supported schools, hospitals, and works of charity. Families built homes and farms that endured across generations. Land was not treated as a disposable asset, but as the setting in which Christian life took root and flourished.

Sacred Scripture consistently presents land as a gift entrusted to human care. In Genesis, man is placed in the garden "to till it and to keep it,"[145] a command that unites cultivation with protection. The earth is not

[145] The Holy Bible, Translated from the Latin Vulgate, Douay-Rheims Edition (Baltimore: John Murphy Company, A.D. 1899), Genesis 2:15.

given for exploitation without limit, but for stewardship. Human beings receive the land not as absolute owners, but as caretakers responsible for preserving its fruitfulness for those who will come after them.

Modern economic systems have increasingly severed this relationship. Land has come to be treated primarily as a speculative instrument within financial markets. Large institutions acquire vast holdings not for habitation or cultivation, but for appreciation and portfolio growth. At the same time, younger generations often find themselves unable to secure homes or farmland, as prices rise beyond the reach of ordinary families.

The consequences of this shift are visible throughout society. Ownership becomes concentrated, communities grow more transient, and the bond between people and place weakens. When land is reduced to a commodity, the stability that once sustained family life and local culture begins to erode. A civilization without rootedness becomes fragile, dependent, and easily disordered.

For this reason, a diocesan Catholic economy must develop structures capable of protecting land from destructive patterns of speculation and fragmentation. One of the most effective instruments for this purpose is the establishment of diocesan land trusts.

A land trust holds property under long-term stewardship for the benefit of the community rather than allowing it to pass continually through speculative markets. Within a Catholic framework, such trusts can preserve farmland, support housing, maintain parish properties, and protect natural resources. The purpose is not to remove land from use, but to ensure that its use remains ordered toward the good of families and the stability of the community.

These trusts can support the development of agricultural systems that supply local food networks, assist young families in securing stable housing, and preserve land for schools, clinics, and charitable institutions. They can also protect forests, waterways, and landscapes whose value cannot be measured solely in economic terms. In doing so, they secure not only resources, but the conditions necessary for a humane and ordered society.

The Church's social teaching has consistently affirmed that the use of land must remain ordered toward the good of the human person and the stability of society. As Fr. Vincent McNabb observed, "the land is God's gift to man, and it is intended for the support of families."[146] Land cannot be reduced to a purely speculative asset without undermining its purpose. Its proper use sustains households, communities, and culture itself. This principle reflects a deeper theological truth. As Fr. Denis Fahey taught, "the organization of economic life must be subordinated to the end for which

[146] Fr. Vincent McNabb, *The Church and the Land* (London: Sheed & Ward, A.D. 1926), Chapter 1.

man was created."[147] Land, like all economic goods, must ultimately serve not only material prosperity but the higher ends of human life.

Recent teaching has further emphasized the moral responsibility owed to creation. The careless destruction of land, the pollution of soil and water, and the depletion of natural resources represent failures not only of prudence, but of justice. A society that consumes its inheritance without regard for the future undermines its own foundations.

These concerns are not merely environmental. They are civilizational. When land is degraded, when agriculture becomes unsustainable, and when communities lose access to stable property, the conditions necessary for human flourishing begin to collapse. A culture cannot endure without a physical foundation capable of sustaining it.

Within the *Catholic Action* framework proposed in this book, land trusts form one of the enduring pillars of long-term stability. Financial systems may fluctuate, political structures may change, and economic conditions may rise and fall. Land held responsibly for the benefit of families and institutions provides a continuity that outlasts these variations.

The stewardship of land also reinforces the broader economic life of the community. Farms sustain local production. Housing supports family formation. Parish lands provide space for education, labor, and charity.

---

[147] Fr. Denis Fahey, *The Mystical Body of Christ in the Modern World* (Dublin: Browne and Nolan, A.D. 1935), Chapter 3.

Natural landscapes preserve both resources and beauty, shaping the environment in which culture develops.

In this way, the land trust becomes more than a financial instrument. It becomes a safeguard of civilization itself. By protecting land from fragmentation and directing its use toward the common good, Catholic communities establish a foundation capable of sustaining their life across generations.

From this foundation, the question of public life naturally arises. No civilization can remain entirely private. The final section considers how Catholic communities may engage the political structures that shape the broader society in which they live.

Catholic Political Influence

✠ ✠ ✠

No civilization can endure if its institutions remain entirely detached from the political order in which it exists. Laws shape the conditions under which families live, businesses operate, schools educate, and churches worship. For this reason, the renewal of Catholic civilization cannot ignore the political structures that govern society. While the Church herself does not exist to function as a political party, the faithful who live within her must nevertheless assume responsibility for the public life of their city, state, and nation.

Throughout Christian history the relationship between faith and political authority has taken many forms. In some ages Catholic rulers openly acknowledged the authority of the Church and sought to govern in accordance with Christian principles. In other periods the faithful lived under regimes indifferent or even hostile to their beliefs. Yet in every age the responsibility remained the same: to shape public life insofar as possible, defending the dignity of the human person and the moral order upon which society depends.

Sacred Scripture affirms that political authority is not self-justifying, but ordered toward justice. Saint Paul writes that rulers are "God's ministers for good," entrusted with the protection of the innocent and the restraint of evil.[148] When authority fulfills this purpose, society flourishes. When it abandons justice, order gives way to disorder and power loses its legitimacy.

The Church has consistently affirmed the responsibility of the faithful to participate in public life. The Catechism teaches that citizens contribute to the common good by active and responsible engagement in civic affairs.[149] Political participation is not merely a right. It is a moral duty grounded in the responsibility each person bears toward society.

---

[148] The Holy Bible, Translated from the Latin Vulgate, Douay-Rheims Edition (Baltimore: John Murphy Company, A.D. 1899), Romans 13:4.
[149] Catechism of the Catholic Church (Vatican City: Libreria Editrice Vaticana, A.D. 1992), §2239.

For this reason, the *Catholic Action* framework described throughout this book includes the development of organized political cooperation among Catholic communities. A diocesan *Catholic Action* political body can assist in coordinating the civic engagement of the faithful, helping Catholics to act with clarity in supporting policies and leaders that protect the conditions necessary for Christian life.

Such an organization does not exist to advance narrow partisan interests. Its purpose is to defend the fundamental principles upon which a just society depends: the protection of human life, the integrity of the family, the freedom of the Church, and the ability of Catholic institutions to educate, serve, and worship according to their moral convictions.

Political coordination allows Catholic communities to exercise influence proportionate to their presence. In many regions Catholics represent a significant portion of the population, yet their voice remains fragmented. When unified by principle rather than divided by passing interests, their influence becomes both more effective and more constructive.

This engagement must remain ordered toward the common good. Catholic political action does not seek domination, but right order. Laws that protect families, support meaningful work, preserve the dignity of life, and encourage responsible stewardship benefit society as a whole. The good sought is not private advantage, but the flourishing of the entire community.

The Second Vatican Council expressed this responsibility with clarity. The laity, it taught, are called to "renew the temporal order" by directing social, economic, and political life according to the spirit of the Gospel.[150] This work belongs not to a select few, but to all who live their vocation within the world.

As Catholic communities rebuild the economic, educational, and social structures described throughout this book, their capacity to influence public life will naturally increase. Strong institutions form stable communities. Stable communities form capable leaders. Such leaders, shaped by faith and disciplined by responsibility, can serve within public life with clarity and integrity.

This influence need not remain confined to a single diocese. As these structures mature, cooperation among dioceses can extend their reach. Resources may be shared. Knowledge may be transferred. Networks may develop across regions. In this way, the renewal of Catholic civilization can expand gradually, not through sudden upheaval, but through steady and coordinated growth.

Hilaire Belloc observed that "the Church is a perpetually defeated

---

150 Second Vatican Council, *Apostolicam Actuositatem* (Vatican City: Vatican Press, A.D. 1965), §7.

thing which always outlives her conquerors."[151] Civilizations rise and fall, yet the life of the Church endures. The task of each generation is not to invent something new, but to rebuild faithfully what has been handed down.

Civilizations are rarely restored through dramatic revolutions. They are rebuilt through patient labor carried out across generations. Parishes strengthened. Schools renewed. Families supported. Land stewarded. Institutions formed with care and governed with responsibility.

The vision presented in this book is not a rigid program, but a framework rooted in realities that already exist. The parishes stand. The dioceses remain. The faithful possess the talents, skills, and resources necessary to begin this work. What is required is not invention, but coordination. Not novelty, but commitment.

The future of Catholic civilization will not be determined solely by elections, markets, or cultural trends. It will be shaped by the decisions of men and women who choose to order their lives according to the faith they profess.

If those decisions are made with perseverance and clarity, renewal will not remain an abstraction. It will take visible form, built gradually through the ordinary work of faithful people. Parish by parish. Guild by

---

[151] Hilaire Belloc, *The Church and Socialism* (London: Catholic Truth Society, A.D. 1937), Chapter 1.

guild. Generation by generation.

Ending Note

Every civilization rests upon certain assumptions about the nature of man and the purpose of society. Some civilizations believe that the highest good lies in wealth, others in power, others in pleasure, others in the pursuit of novelty and endless change. The Christian civilization that once shaped the West rested upon a very different foundation. It held that the ultimate purpose of human life is not merely prosperity or comfort, but union with God, and that the institutions of society should help guide men and women toward that end.

For many centuries the structures of Christian civilization developed slowly around this conviction. Families formed stable homes. Parishes became the spiritual centers of communities. Guilds organized labor and protected standards of honest work. Monasteries cultivated land, preserved learning, and offered refuge to the poor and the weary. Schools and universities formed the minds of new generations. The cathedral stood at the center of the city, not merely as a place of worship, but as a declaration in stone that man is ordered toward eternity.

No civilization endures forever in its original form. Human societies rise, flourish, decline, and are renewed again in different shapes. Yet the Christian vision of society has never disappeared entirely. Even in periods of political collapse or cultural confusion the Church has continued to preserve the spiritual and institutional seeds from which renewal can grow.

The present age is one of profound transition. The economic, technological, and political systems that shape modern life are developing at extraordinary speed. New tools allow humanity to communicate instantly across continents, to coordinate global networks of production, and to accumulate wealth and knowledge on a scale unknown to earlier generations. At the same time many of the moral and cultural foundations that once guided Western civilization have grown uncertain. Families weaken. Communities fragment. The meaning of the human person is debated in ways that would have seemed unthinkable only a century ago.

In such a moment, the temptation arises either to despair or to retreat into private life, imagining that the forces shaping the modern world are too vast for ordinary people to influence. Yet the history of Christianity suggests a different conclusion. Civilizations are not rebuilt by abstraction or decree. More often they are rebuilt quietly by communities of people who choose to organize their lives around truth.

The Church has done this before.

When the political order of the Roman world began to collapse in the early centuries of the Christian era, it was not emperors or armies that preserved the foundations of Western civilization. It was bishops who continued to shepherd their dioceses, monks who cultivated land and copied manuscripts, craftsmen who maintained the standards of their trades, and families who continued to raise children in the faith.

From these humble and often unnoticed efforts, a new civilization slowly emerged.

The purpose of this book has been to explore how something similar might occur again in the modern age. The structures described in these pages are not inventions drawn from abstract theory. They are adaptations of institutions that once formed the backbone of Christian society. Dioceses, parishes, guilds, charitable institutions, schools, and systems of mutual aid once formed an integrated social order. They can do so again.

What is required today is not the creation of entirely new institutions but the renewal and coordination of those that already exist.

The diagram presented on the next page offers a visual representation of that coordination. At its center stands the *Catholic Action Executive Council*, responsible for guiding the collaboration of the laity under the spiritual authority of the bishop. Surrounding it are the major boards responsible for law, economic development, education, healthcare, security, certification standards, youth formation, and the cultural life of the Church. From these boards flow the three great chambers of Catholic society: the

Chamber of Collegiate Guilds, the *Chamber of Labor Guilds*, and the *Chamber of Charitable Associations*.

The purpose of this structure is not bureaucracy. It is cooperation. It provides a framework through which the many talents already present within the Catholic community can begin to work together rather than in isolation.

To understand what such coordination might look like in practice, imagine the life of a child born within a society where *Catholic Action* is functioning as intended.

A child is born to a Catholic mother and father and baptized in the parish church. His early years are shaped by a stable family, a parish community, and schools that understand their mission not merely as academic instruction but as the formation of the whole person forming both intellect and character. Through Catholic education he learns not only mathematics and science, but also the languages, literature, philosophy, and history that form the cultural inheritance of the Christian West.

He knows the saints. He knows the story of the Church. He knows the geography of the world and the history of his own people, and truths that give coherence to human life.

His education is supported by a political and civic framework that defends the freedom of Catholic institutions to operate and educates families through systems such as school choice and vouchers secured through Catholic civic organization. In his adolescence he participates in youth associations connected to *Catholic Action*, where he forms friendships and develops habits of service and leadership.

During his education he encounters mentors from various guilds who introduce him to different vocations. Some pursue trades, others professions, others religious life. Because the society around him values both intellectual and manual work, each path is treated with dignity.

When he reaches adulthood, he chooses his vocation freely, supported by institutions that reinforce rather than undermine that choice. If he is called to married life, he marries a woman formed by the same culture of faith. Their wedding reception takes place within a network of Catholic businesses and institutions that support the life of the community.

When the young couple seeks to purchase a home, they do so through Catholic professionals who share their values. A Catholic real estate agent guides them through the process. Their mortgage is issued through a diocesan credit union or cooperative lending system. Their home is built by construction companies and tradesmen connected to the labor guilds, firms that follow ethical standards of fair wages and just contracts.

Their employment also takes place within a network of Catholic enterprises. Their healthcare is provided through systems that respect the dignity of human life. Their retirement savings are managed by financial advisors who invest according to Catholic moral standards rather than in industries that contradict the teachings of the Church.

Their daily lives remain connected to the broader Catholic community through modern tools such as diocesan websites, digital directories, and community networks that allow them to find services, employment opportunities, cultural events, and charitable initiatives within the life of their diocese.

Their labor is supported by guild associations that provide training, mentorship, and representation. Their food comes from producers who operate according to ethical standards verified by the Benedictus Seal, a certification that assures Catholic families that the goods they purchase are produced with just labor, moral integrity, and fair pricing.

Their parish remains the center of their spiritual life, but it is no longer isolated from the rest of society. The parish stands within a network of schools, farms, businesses, charities, and cultural institutions that together form a living Christian community.

This example is only one illustration. In reality, every diocese would develop its own particular form according to its population, resources, and culture. Yet the principle remains the same. *Catholic Action* seeks to reconnect the many dimensions of life that modern society has separated.

Faith, work, family, culture, and community once again become parts of a single civilization.

None of this will emerge instantly. Civilizations grow slowly, just as trees grow slowly. The cathedral builders of the Middle Ages often began their work knowing that the final stones might not be laid for generations. They built anyway, trusting that the future would continue the work they had begun.

The same spirit is required now.

Ending Note

The renewal of Christian civilization will not come through a single movement, a single program, or a single generation. It will come through the steady labor of men and women who choose to build institutions that reflect the truths they profess.

A young family chooses to remain rooted in their parish community rather than drifting endlessly from place to place. A craftsman trains an apprentice in both skill and integrity. A group of professionals organizes a guild that supports ethical business practices. A parish restores its sacred music and renews its cultural life. A community protects farmland and develops housing so that young families can remain close to one another.

None of these actions appear dramatic in isolation. Yet over time they form the quiet architecture of civilization.

The task before the Church in America is not merely to resist decline, but to be creative and build. Catholics are called not only to preserve the fragments of the past, but to create structures capable of sustaining the faith in the future.

If the vision described in these pages encourages even a small number of communities to begin that work, its purpose will have been fulfilled.

Civilizations are not restored through moments of enthusiasm. They are restored through fidelity, discipline, and perseverance across generations.

The Church has carried those truths for two thousand years.

The question that now stands before the faithful is whether we are willing to build the structures that allow those truths to shape the world once again.

ABOUT THE AUTHOR

C. A. Chuba, known personally as **Corey Alan Chuba**, was born in Butler, Pennsylvania, and has spent his life rooted in the cultural and civic life of the Pittsburgh region. He served in the Pennsylvania Army National Guard and Army Reserves, earned a Master of Business Administration, and built his professional career in the corporate banking sector, while also pursuing entrepreneurial and nonprofit work.

A devoted husband and father, Chuba's interests include archery hunting, winemaking, gardening, and the study of classical literature, history, philosophy, theology, and geopolitics. He strives to order his life according to the Latin maxim *Omnia sunt sicut Deus vult* — "All is as God wills it."

www.ingramcontent.com/pod-product-compliance
Lightning Source LLC
LaVergne TN
LVHW091138080826
845145LV00008B/2189

* 9 7 8 1 9 6 7 4 7 0 1 7 4 *